OPEN YOUR HEART

with *Winter Fitness*

"With anecdotes, inspiration and hard facts, Lisa Marie Mercer encourages and inspires readers—especially mid-life readers—to get out and enjoy winter, whether to nurture, to heal, or just to have fun. In addition to motivational words, she offers specifics on how to go about becoming a skier."

—Claire Walter, Ski and Snow Sports Author
www.claire-walter.com

"*Open Your Heart with Winter Fitness* is a delightful book. It will make you a better skier, guaranteed. And it might just make you a better person along the way."

—Dr. Harry Lodge, author of *Younger Next Year*

"The "magic" of skiing happens when the mind, body, and spirit are unified. The healthier and more fit we are when we enter the experience, the greater our odds for the "magic." Lisa's book is an excellent guide."

—Tom Crum, Director, "The Magic of Skiing" (Aspen, CO); Author of *Three Deep Breaths, Journey to Center* and *The Magic of Conflict*
www.thomascrum.com

"I've just read a copy of Lisa Mercer's book, *Open Your Heart with Winter Fitness*, and I'm just delighted with it. She brings two incredibly powerful pieces to this chaotic skiing table: (1) her fresh and humble newness to the sport—if you are a new or intermediate skier, you will love this book; and (2) her thorough mastery of creating accessible fitness for recreational athletes. If you are a new, intermediate or expert skier, you need this book. It will hold an honored position in my ski library, and I will recommend it to my students."

—Weems Westfeldt, Ancient Ski Pro,
Ski & Snowboard Schools of Aspen, author of *Brilliant Skiing*

"Thank you, Lisa Marie Mercer, for this fresh and relevant look into skiing fitness. *Open Your Heart with Winter Fitness* is comprehensive, fun and informative for every level skier—from the entry-level beginner to the instructor."

—Deb Armstrong, Olympic Gold Medalist,
Giant Slalom, Sarajevo 1984, PSIA Alpine Team Member
www.debbiearmstrong.com

OPEN YOUR HEART

with *Winter Fitness*

Mastering Life Through Love of the Slopes

LISA MARIE MERCER

DreamTime Publishing, Inc.

978-1-60166-002-2

Library of Congress Control Number: 2006931925

Trademarks used herein are for the benefit of the respective trademark owners.

Branding, website, and cover design for DreamTime Publishing by
    Rearden Killion • www.reardenkillion.com
Illustrations by Janice Marie Phelps • www.janicephelps.com
Manuscript consulting by Jeannette Cézanne • www.customline.com
Text layout and design by Gary A. Rosenberg • www.garyarosenberg.com

This publication is designed to provide accurate and authoritative information in regard to the subject matter covered. It is sold with the understanding that the publisher is not engaged in rendering legal, accounting, or other professional service. If legal advice or other expert assistance is required, the services of a competent professional person should be sought.

—*From a declaration of principles jointly adopted by a committee of the American Bar Association and a committee of publishers.*

Readers should consult with a physician before undertaking any exercise, fitness, or diet program.

This book is printed on recycled, acid-free paper containing a minimum of 50% recycled, de-inked fiber.

Contents

PART TWO: Body (The Snow Condition Workout)

Appendices

Note from the Publisher

Balancing the overall mission of a series of books with each author's individual creativity and vision is an enjoyable and rewarding challenge. The goal of this note is to tie the loose ends together to make your experience with this book as meaningful as possible.

We have two goals with the *Open Your Heart* series. One is to provide you with practical advice about your hobby or interest, in this case winter fitness and snow sports. We trust this advice will increase your ongoing enjoyment of these activities, or perhaps even encourage you to rediscover your childhood love of playing in the snow.

Our second goal is to help you use what you know and love to make the rest of your life happier and easier. This process worked in different ways for each of our writers, so it will likely work in different ways for each of you. For some, it's a matter of becoming more self-aware. Just realizing what makes you happy on the slopes, and then gradually learning to use those feelings as a barometer when dealing with your job, relationships, and other issues could be an important first step. For others, snow sports provide an important outlet for stress and contemplation, allowing you to go back into your daily life refreshed. For yet others, you might discover how to meditate, how to connect with the mysterious flow of the Universe when you are immersed in your winter fitness activities. Once you recognize the beauty of that for what it is, you can then learn to connect with the flow in other ways at other times.

We are not suggesting you will find all of your answers in this book. We are, though, inviting you to look at something you love with new eyes, a new perspective, and a new heart. Once you recognize the importance of feeling good in one area of your life, you are open to feeling good in the rest of your life. And that is the cornerstone to mastering your life.

Happy reading!

Meg Bertini
Publisher

In memory of Kay Bailey
(May 6, 1947–July 5, 2006).

May you spread your joy of skiing
throughout the slopes of heaven.

Acknowledgments

I could write an entire book about the people who have "opened my heart" and inspired me to a write a book about winter fitness. These are just a few of them.

A heartfelt thanks goes to the forum members of EpicSki.com for their encouragement, inspiration—and for putting up with my cyber-temper tantrums! All of us at EpicSki owe enormous gratitude to Joan Rostad for taking on the burden of forming and organizing the EpicSki Academy. It was Joan who challenged me to write an article about ski fitness, thus initiating the turn of events that would eventually add the words "professional writer" to my résumé.

I am particularly in deep gratitude to Weems Westfeldt for showing me the beauty of brilliant skiing and for being the visual embodiment of what brilliant skiing looks like.

Whether on the slopes, the stage or in print, friend and mentor Michael Martorano never accepted any work that fell short of my potential. Thank you for believing in me, for taking care of me when I was hurt, and for bandaging my ego when my spirit was broken.

This book would not exist without the help of Meg Bertini, whose inspiration to create DreamTime Publishing inspired the dreamer in all of her authors.

Finally, Mark Mercer, my beloved husband and soul mate, took my whimsical fantasy of a studio in the mountains and turned it into a reality. Thank you for your unconditional love and for continuing to believe in me when I let you down. I want to be on mountains with you when we are older.

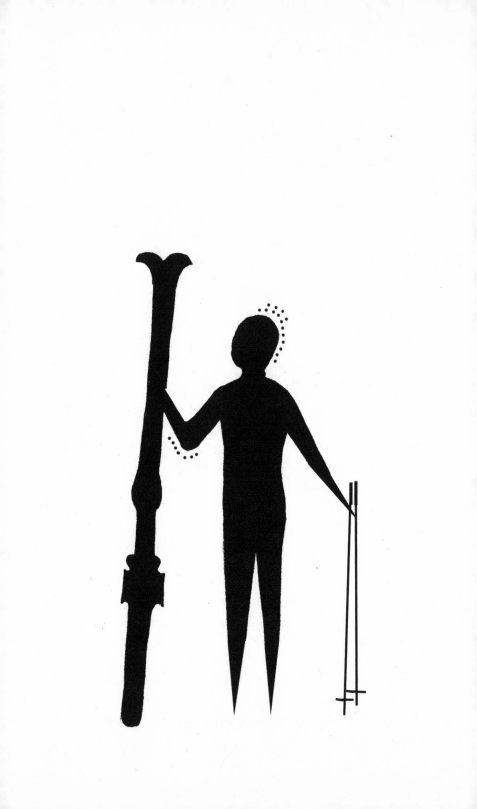

Preface

Peruse the shelves of any bookstore, and you will find a variety of books on winter sports, exercise, and health. Wander over to the self-help section, and you will see thousands of books that tell you how to make your life a little bit better. The snow sport books tell you how to learn a snow sport, the exercise books promise to make your body beautiful, and the self-help books hint at a more beautiful life.

While putting them all together is an ambitious endeavor, where are we when we deprive ourselves of dreams and ambition? Thus, in writing this book, I have illustrated how learning a snow sport can enhance other aspects of your life, and how committing to a fitness routine that supports that sport can have a profound affect on your confidence and state of mind. It represents an integration of body, mind, and sport.

Enjoy!

PART ONE

Sport, Mind, and Spirit

INTRODUCTION

How to Use This Book and Turning Points

We teach best what we need to learn.

—RICHARD BACH

As I mentioned in the preface, this book is a highly ambitious endeavor. In writing it, I have attempted to do the impossible: Please all of the people, all of the time. So there are a number of ways to use this book.

My primary goal in writing *Open Your Heart with Winter Fitness: Mastering Life Through Love of the Slopes* is to inspire my readers to become people for all seasons. Throughout the book, you will hear me talk a good deal about skiing. That's because skiing happens to be my passion. Even if you never intend to go to a ski area, however, the workouts in Part Two will give you the physical agility that will allow you to enjoy—rather than fight with—the winter season. Imagine having the balance skills to be able to go out for a run or a long walk on a snowy winter day. Winter without weight gain. Now there's a thought!

Yet my purpose goes beyond avoiding weight gain, although I do admit it is a worthy cause. The ability to accept and embrace all four seasons, and be physically, mentally, and spiritually prepared for them is a precious gift. Hopefully once you have the physical tools to prepare your body for the winter season, your physical being will encourage your mind and spirit to join in the enthusiasm.

If you are already a snow-sliding enthusiast, but have no interest in this mental/spiritual stuff, you can skip ahead to Part Two, where you will find an abundance of snow sport-specific workouts. Throughout the entire book, however, I have included a good deal of hardcore research about why this type of fitness plan is effective. Knowledge, as they say, is power. In providing you with detailed fitness research, I have hopefully empowered you to make intelligent choices regarding your sport-specific workouts. That empowerment in itself can be exhilarating. The ability to make informed choices about what your body needs on any given day is priceless.

Many readers who are new to snow-sliding sports may be having issues with that four-letter f-word associated with them. I'm talking about *fear*, of course! While there have been a number of excellent books written about fear on the slopes, most of them involve mental exercises that can only be performed on the hills. The physical exercises in this book will give you the opportunity to explore your fears in a safer environment. There's an added benefit: You can practice them all year round. Conquering fear in sport can have a profound effect on the rest of your life as well. I've also included a glossary at the back of the book to help explain unfamiliar terminology.

I hear some of you saying, "Sport, *shmort*, I just want to tone my butt and gut!" Not a problem. The stability ball, Bosu, and resistance band exercises are some of the most effective workouts on the market, and we all know that when you look better, you feel better. On the other hand, some readers may be interested in a mind/body fitness technique that does not involve performing contortions while chanting unintelligible Hindu phrases. With this in mind, I've illustrated ways to bring a mind/body approach to the more modern forms of exercise. Even if you aren't interested in the workouts per se, I invite you to explore the ways that gliding down a snow-covered hill can induce a meditative state.

Another group of readers might be seeking inspiration from "everyday people." Magazines and books are filled with anecdotes about the trials and tribulations of the superstars. Each day, however, small but attainable miracles of transformation happen to us common folks. Here is my story.

TURNING POINTS

Once upon a time, I was the quintessential city woman. Having essentially grown up on the subways in the heart and soul of New York City, I knew the score about all things urban. After all, I am a native New Yorker!

At eighteen, I joined a fitness center as an excuse to avoid the ever-present drug scene that prevailed on college campuses in the 1970s. By age nineteen, I became a fitness instructor. Eventually, I began to live for my workouts. I ran my first marathon when I was thirty and continued to train at marathon intensity year-round. I continued to train at this intensity, even though I was teaching one to three aerobic classes daily and spending at least two hours a day in the weight room.

Running was my only outdoor activity. I loved it in the spring, summer, and fall, but hated it in the winter. In fact, I despised the winter season. Each year when the clocks were turned back, my mood would darken. I believe that this condition is called Seasonal Affective Disorder, or SAD.

While I loved the New York City nightlife, my winter sadness caused me to hibernate during the colder days. Perhaps this was why it took me until age thirty-four to meet my soul mate. One night, we walked along a moonlit beach on Block Island. In the distance, a band was playing *Let Me Call You Sweetheart*. I told him that I wanted to be on beaches with him when we were old. He asked me to marry him. Of course I said yes.

Although Mark and I had, and continue to have, a good deal in common, there was one major difference: Mark loved to ski. One of the many points of contention in his first marriage was his ex-wife's refusal to ski, as well as her desire to live in a perpetually warmer climate. Beaches began fading from my fantasy future.

Before long, Mark asked me to join him on a ski trip. My first thought was, "Are you out of your mind?" Since I believed that New York City was already in the Arctic Zone, I could not understand why anyone in his or her right mind would want to go to Vermont in the middle of the winter. I had nightmares of being eternally frozen, never to return to the comfort of the weight room and elliptical machine. Nonetheless, Mark was a keeper, so I agreed to ski by my man.

On the bus ride to Killington, Vermont, I tried to hypnotize myself with affirmations.

I am strong.

I am invincible.

I am a fitness instructor.

I am a marathon runner.

I am scared out of my wits!

I showed up on the slopes the next morning in my form-fitting ski outfit, feeling a bit full of myself since I looked better than some of the twenty-somethings in the ski class. My pride would be short-lived. How should I describe this unfortunate incident? Did you see the film, *Bridget Jones, the Edge of Reason?* Do you remember the ski resort scene? Compared to me, Bridget was the famous ski racer Picabo Street.

Despite my extreme strength, flexibility and aerobic endurance, I could not stay up on my skis for more than one minute. A group of handsome ski instructors were lined up across the mountain, looking like a bunch of Chippendales. I somehow managed to fall face-down across their skis, as if offering myself as a sacrifice to the gods. For my next trick, I skied into another ski class, knocking them all down. I was having a really hard time winning friends and influencing people. Every time I tried to get up, *boom,* down went the Baby Boomer.

It would be twelve years until I agreed to be coerced into giving it a second try.

By then, we were living in Boston. I had started teaching classes in Pilates and stability ball. I no longer ran marathons, and was not spending even half as much time in the weight room as I had in my younger days.

It was New Year's Day. Mark's children were visiting from Florida, and we were going to Vermont. Since I did not want to be left in the room with nothing to do, I agreed to accompany them to Mount Snow. Somehow I got talked into taking a lesson. That day, the temperature was fifteen degrees below zero.

Although I still looked good for my age, I was uncomfortably aware that at age forty-five, I was considerably older than anyone else in the class. I told the instructor about my past failure at the sport, as well as my concern that I was just too darned old for this stuff. He asked me what I did for a living. I described the stability ball classes that I taught. "That sounds terrifying," he said. I laughed so hard that I began to glide.

Of course, gliding is what it's all about.

It was frightening at first. But then I began to allow the mountain to be my dancing partner as it led me down the hill. Songs like Sinatra's *Nice and Easy Does It* played through my mind, providing me with a rhythm and an affirmation. I was oh so free, yet surprisingly in control.

Soon it was time for Lisa's first lift ride. Despite the fact that I had not fallen once during the lesson, I was still feeling apprehensive. My lift mate didn't help much. She was saying her Hail Marys. Deciding that I could use all the help I could get, I joined in.

When I find myself in times of trouble
Mother Mary moves my skis . . .

When we got off the lift, our ski instructor looked as if he was about to have a heart attack. We had apparently crisscrossed our skis with each other and had still somehow managed to ski off the exit ramp without falling.

How was it that this older woman, infinitely less fit than her younger self, had managed to do better at the sport on the second time around? The answer is simple. The newer modalities I'd added to my teaching repertoire incorporated some of the most important elements of ski fitness: Balance, coordination, agility, postural alignment, and proprioception.

My former fitness methods involved predictable exercises. Absolutely nothing, though, that happens on a ski slope is predictable. For that matter, nothing in *life* is predictable. When you train on a stability ball or any other balance device, you need to react to the ball's movements with spontaneity and agility.

This sort of balance and proprioception has a direct carry-over to the slopes. Ski instructors call this concept "teaching for transfer." Little did I know that this sense of spontaneity would carry over into the rest of my life.

The people we love the most are often the ones that inspire us to develop new hobbies. Dawna Markova, author of *I Will Not Die an Unlived Life*, asks us to consider this question:

"What do you truly love? To explore this question, it's helpful to go back to the seeds of your loving and ahead of the fruit you'd like to bear in the world. Who taught you to see beauty in the world? Who believed in you no matter what? Who was a great soul for you, an inspiring companion, who passed on to you a wonder and love of some aspect of being alive?"

Without a doubt, Mark was the person I truly loved. To this day, I am forever grateful to him for inspiring me to become involved in this beautiful sport.

Epilogue: Five years after that day at Mount Snow, Mark and I packed our van with our greyhound, two cats, and a variety of balance and sport training toys. We moved to Summit County, Colorado, where we opened Mountain Sport Pilates and Fitness.

When we first moved to Colorado, I "came home to a place I'd never been before" as the song would say. Having spent most of my life in the black-and-white urban metropolises of New York and Boston, this Technicolor mountain community provided me with things once conspicuous by their absence in my life.

These days, as I awaken each morning and go to my window, I wonder what the mountains will wear today. You see, they like to change their colors with their mood. Sometimes they dress in purple. At times they dress in green. As autumn approaches, the aspens turn golden, reflecting the bright Colorado sun. They embellish the mountain like ornaments on a Christmas tree, reminding the locals that winter, their favorite season, is on its way. Then, surprise, Santa comes early, and we get a September sprinkling of snow. The town reverberates with joy and anticipation.

As night falls, the colors of daylight blend slowly with the darker colors of the night. I am living in a watercolor painting; but this painting is my reality. This is Summit County, where we embrace the challenges along with the beauty that each of our seasons graciously offers us. "When you feel down, look up." We say this to people when we notice that they seem sad.

During the winter, Mark teaches at the Breckenridge Ski Resort, and I work part-time as a skier surveyor for Copper Mountain. One day, I walked into the cafeteria, and saw a beautiful, fit, forty-something woman sitting by herself. As I approached, I noticed that she was in tears. Apparently, even though she was in incredible shape, this skiing thing just did not agree with her. Yet like a woman who is helplessly in love with a reluctant suitor, something was drawing her to the sport. She longed for the thrill and excitement of alpine skiing but was afraid it was unattainable.

I didn't take many surveys that day. Instead, I sat down and told her my story, and advised her about what she can do to tweak her fitness routine to make it more ski-specific. For her, and anyone who believes that age is just a number, this book is for you!

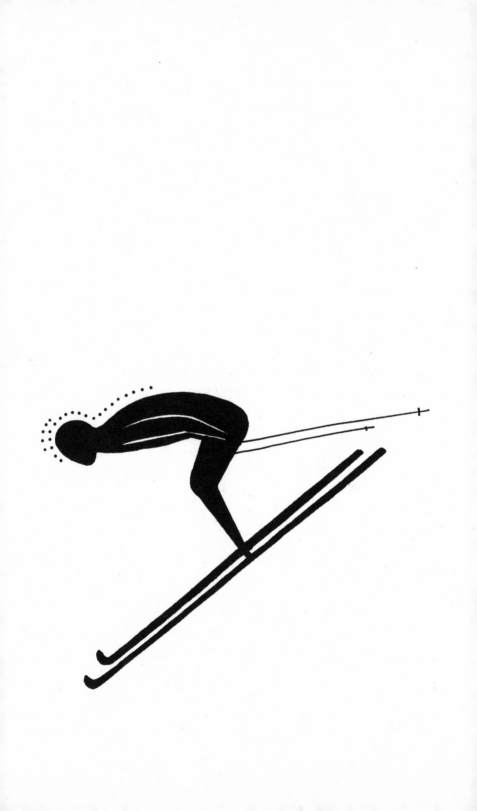

ONE

Going Downhill and Loving It!

The pleasure of risk is in the control needed to ride it with
assurance so that what appears dangerous to the outsider is,
to the participant, simply a matter of intelligence, skill,
intuition, coordination—in a word, experience.

—A. ALVEREZ

The baby boomers of today have a true understanding of the word "fitness." Some even say that they popularized the fitness movement. A recent article in the *New York Times*, however, referred to a condition called "Boomeritis." Apparently the over-forty crowd has been spending a good deal of time and money in the orthopedist's office. Although their fitness levels are still quite high, with age, if left unchallenged, balance and coordination begin to falter. The corporate life leads to postural misalignment that in turn causes muscular imbalance. These imbalances impede technique and make a middle-aged snow-sport enthusiast more susceptible to injury. Is this inevitable? Not with the right fitness plan.

In 1993, the well-known ski coach Warren Witherell published his masterpiece, *The Athletic Skier*. In chapter two, he lists the ten most important traits that are most apparent in athletic skiers. Exceptional balance is at the top of the list.

According to Witherell, "You must strive for perfect balance.

Good balance is never good enough. Accept no compromise. Perfect balance makes optimum performance possible. Imperfect balance inhibits performance." In Witherell's memory, balance exercises will be an important element of this book.

While today's baby boomers are the first generation of serious exercisers, they have only recently begun to explore the idea of "balanced fitness." Although you will no longer find them in sweatbands and leg warmers, they have stayed faithful to the fitness lifestyle. As a result, they refuse to get old. While some are eternal gym rats, others have used their fitness benefits as a means of enjoying the great outdoors.

Evidence of this can be found on any given day at Copper, Colorado, where you will see a number of athletic folks in red jackets leading large groups of people down some of the most challenging trails on the mountain. From a distance, you might believe that they are a group of skiers in their twenties and thirties. Their body movements defy their age. They are, of course, the Over the Hill Gang, a national organization of skiers and active people over the age of forty-five. Some have been skiing for all of their lives. Others have taken up the sport in their forties, fifties, and even in their sixties. For some, this new activity is just another sport in their repertoire of activities. For others, it signifies a rebirth that inspires them to change their life and lifestyles, while aspiring to even greater accomplishments.

Even professional athletes understand the benefits of learning a new sport as an adult. Consider the words of former Olympic ski racer Martin Bell: "I was lucky enough to learn to ski as a child, but I learned to snowboard as an adult. So I know how much more difficult it is to take up any sport at a later stage in life. Nevertheless, I firmly believe that it is never too late to discover the brilliant white winter world of skiing. And with some good instruction, and plenty of time and commitment, it is possible to improve at any age. Last year, I skied with a client who had started skiing two years ago, while in his fifties. Already he can enjoy the wonderful floating sensation of making short, linked turns in the fall-line in deep powder."

I was astonished to discover that Lito Tejada Flores, one of the most renowned experts in the ski industry, did not learn to ski until after college:

"When are you too old to learn to ski? When are you too old to smile? To hike, to hug your best friend? A round-about way of saying: never. Many skiers are envious of those who started skiing young, really young, too long ago to even remember, and who today ski as easily and thoughtlessly as they breathe. Not me, I learned to ski after college and I remember that first winter on skis as if it were yesterday. The excitement, the frustrations, the victories, my first day in deep powder, the whole process of making friends with these slippery sticks, with snow, with winter, with steep mountainsides.

"Learning to ski is not drudge-work; it's an adventure. An adventure that's a prelude to many other adventures, other seasons, other mountains. As adults we bring our complicated, often conflicted selves to the ski slopes. And putting on skis we face our anxieties, test our limits, discover strengths and build skills we didn't even suspect we were capable of. How could one possibly spend a better day, weekend, or vacation than flying down a snow covered mountain. Say goodbye to gravity. Say hello to winter. Don't look back."

While this is certainly an inspiration, the midlife mind and body can pose unique challenges to both novices and aficionados of any snow sport. At times, the proverbial spirit is willing, but the body rebels. Then again, the body may be ready, but the mind cannot make the leap of faith. In some cases, even the fittest of the forty-somethings may be challenged by the balance and coordination skills required for the sport.

As the baby boomers grow older, fitness professionals seek new ways to develop conditioning programs that suit their needs. Although alpine skiing or any other snow sport would not be considered fitness techniques, they have their own physical and psychological benefits. After learning a winter sport, people who once suffered from seasonal affective disorder (SAD) often look forward to winter. Cold tolerance is improved, as well as balance. As much as we *ooh* and *ah* when we see Bode Miller recovering from a near wipe-out, it is equally as impressive to see a seventy-year-old walk across an icy base area in ski boots without falling down.

Am I actually telling you that learning a snow sport as an adult may in fact be a healthy thing to do? You bet. Aside from being a great way to improve your balance (as a weight-bearing activity that is performed on unpredictable surfaces), participating in a winter sport can also prevent osteoporosis. In fact, since it is often pretty sunny in ski areas, you are actually getting a double dose of osteoporosis prevention. The healing rays of natural sunlight are responsible for generating vitamin D, which prevents osteoporosis, breast cancer, prostate cancer, psoriasis, and depression. Since cold weather often keeps us indoors during the winter, many of us suffer from vitamin D deficiency. Engaging in a winter sport is probably the most fun you will ever have while doing things that are great for your health.

Learning a snow sport can also have a profound effect on your creativity. Even though John Denver wrote *Annie's Song* for his wife, he was inspired to write the words "you fill up my senses" while looking down from a ski lift. As many of us learn when we move here, the mountains have the capacity to inspire. Not only do they inspire creativity, they inspire the courage—or chutzpah, if you will—to set this creativity in motion. In other words, creativity becomes dynamic. Just as skiing or any other snow sport coaxes us to come outside to play, the mountains entice us to bring our inner creative life into the great outdoors. Before you know it, creative ideas turn into creative actions, and actions become lifestyles.

Action. Now there's a word. I once interviewed Gary Ketzenbarger, probably one of Summit County's most talented actor/directors. When he's not performing or directing at the Lake Dillon Theatre, Gary teaches t'ai chi and works as a dog-sled guide. I asked if he saw a connection between his outdoor activities and his work on the stage. He answered that both of these activities are about action.

When we moved to Colorado, I began to take ski lessons from an instructor who was also an actor and director. Michael Martorano is another example of someone who was moved by the mountains. He had a relatively successful acting career when he lived in New York City. When he learned to ski in his early forties, however, he was inspired to find a way that he could share this fantastic activity with others. When he discovered that Summit County has an active theatre community, he decided to move here.

Ironically, I was one of the few creative New Yorkers who never aspired to be an actress. Mike, however, often carries ideas from the acting world onto the slopes. For example, one of his major goals was to change my attitude on the slopes from *No* to *Go!* As I began to play with this idea, on the hill and in my life, I happened to notice that the local theatre was holding auditions for J.R. Gurney's *Love Letters*. I found myself intrigued by the Melissa Gardner character, a sort of artistic daredevil who, as a child, would ski the more challenging slopes at a ski area against her parents' wishes. Later, as an adult, she writes to the other character in the play, telling him that she is in Aspen.

"What are you doing in Aspen?" he asked.
"Going steadily downhill," she replied.

This phrase, going steadily downhill, became my mantra on the ski slopes. As I began to explore my "inner Melissa" while skiing, I felt that I understood the character enough to audition for the role. To make a long story short, I got the part.

With a considerable amount of talent in our midst, the Summit County drama scene is hardly traditional community theater. What prompted me to even think that I could audition for a show? In even auditioning, I was taking the risk of ridicule. From taking risks on the slopes, however, I had developed a bit of chutzpah!

SKIING AND THE FINE ART OF CHUTZPAH

Chutzpah once had a negative connotation. Since becoming part of the American vernacular, however, it is often considered an admirable trait. Here are some of the popular synonyms for chutzpah:

- Cheekiness
- Nerve
- Daring

The Finnish use the word *sisu* to describe these qualities. Roughly translated, *sisu* means strength of will, determination, perseverance, and acting rationally in the face of adversity. It is interesting to note that similar concepts exist amongst other people—the Inuit cultures, for example—whose habitats are cold environments.

Sisu goes beyond the concepts of bravery and strength. It implies an ability to finish the task and get things done. Perhaps chutzpah and *sisu* are codependent concepts. Chutzpah gives you the nerve to accept and complete the task at hand, no matter how challenging it may seem. *Sisu* gives you the determination to carry it out.

Sisu is a quality I see in many snow-sport enthusiasts. Miraculously, it seems to carry over from their sport into their daily lives. My ski friends seem to epitomize the saying that tough times don't last, tough people do. People with snow-sport *sisu* share a significant bond. Within this bond there are no age boundaries.

I recently had a rather humorous experience. I was chatting with a bunch of cyber friends on the EpicSki.com forum when, as often happens in cyberspace, we went off-topic. I started talking about seeing the movie *The Last Waltz*. Although I had "come of age" in the 1970s, somehow I had never seen that film until this year.

One young forum member, who goes by the name of Moguljunkie, commented that he wished that he had known the members of The Band when they lived near him in Woodstock, New York. This triggered a memory.

Step into the *Way Back Machine* and travel with me to the late 1970s. I am in the car with my friends Monique and Alan and their two kids, Adam and Nicole. We are driving from New York City to their home in Woodstock, New York. As we get closer to the town of Woodstock, *The Last Waltz* is playing on the car tape deck. The kids are upset. They don't want their friends to hear them playing this "hippie music." Go figure.

I decided to tell this story on the forum. A few hours later, Moguljunkie replied. "I know that guy Adam. As a matter of fact, I *am* Adam." I got back in touch with his mother, with whom I had not spoken in about twelve years. She was astonished that I had decided to take up skiing. "I can't believe it. You were the only other person I knew who was as big a chicken as I was. Now you're going down big mountains on skinny sticks and hanging out in cyberspace with my son!" If you're looking for the fountain of youth, you just might find it on the mountains.

YES, VIRGINIA!

Actress Virginia Madsen can also tell you a thing or two about the relationship between learning to snow-slide and *sisu*. Suffering from a severe case of postpartum depression, Madsen felt that she was a Hollywood has-been and was pessimistic about future prospects for her acting career. To make matters worse, one day she stumbled on the sidewalk and injured her neck. Although her doctor prescribed pain medication and bed rest for the pain, her spirit was not healing. Eventually she decided to practice Pilates and other forms of exercise.

Her turning-point was when she was asked to participate in a celebrity ski event. Although she did not ski, the event organizers sweetened the deal by assigning two stud-muffin ski instructors to coach her. In the middle of the race, she suffered an unfortunate faceplant on the mountain. At first, she was discouraged; then she got up and finished the race. For the next few days, Madsen practiced from the moment the lifts opened until they closed. A few days later, one of her instructors saw her looking down from the top of a Black Diamond run. He told her that if she could learn how to ski it, she could walk into any audition free of fear. When she got home, she decided that if she could "hurl herself down the mountain" she could "hurl herself back into life."

GLIDING WITH THE FLOW

Although this is an inspiring story, I find it interesting to observe which people end up enjoying the skiing experience and which people continue to dislike it. The answer can possibly be explained in two words: flow state.

Psychology professor Mihaly Csikszentmihalyi developed the

Mihaly Csikszentmihalyi was the former head of the department of psychology at the University of Chicago. His work Flow: The Psychology of Optimal Experience expresses his theory that people are happiest when they are in a state of flow—a Zen-like state of total oneness with the activity at hand. There are eight essential components that influence Flow State:

1. Clear goals

2. Concentration and focus

3. A loss of the feeling of self-consciousness

4. Distorted sense of time

5. Direct and immediate feedback

6. Balance between ability level and challenge

7. A sense of personal control over the situation or activity.

8. The activity is intrinsically rewarding, so there is an effortlessness of action.

concept of flow. In his book *Flow: The Psychology of Optimal Experience,* he describes flow as being a Zen-like state of oneness with the activity you are performing. In an interview with *Wired* magazine, he describes the flow experience as "being completely involved in an activity for its own sake. The ego falls away. Time flies. Every action, movement, and thought follows inevitably from the previous one, like playing jazz. Your whole being is involved, and you're using your skills to the utmost."

In *Flow in Sports,* author Susan Jackson speaks about factors that influence the "flow states" in athletic activity. One of these is the challenge/skills factor. In order for the flow state to happen, the athlete must be engaged in an activity that is challenging enough to be exciting, but not so challenging as to cause anxiety.

Many people in their midyears feel that they are not capable of developing the skills needed to become proficient at any type of snow sliding. This is often complicated by the fact that motor learning skills might be slower as we get older. Since the winter sport season is short, there is only a limited amount of practice time. Thus, they sometimes alternate between being bored on the bunny slopes and scared out of their wits on the Black Diamonds. A year-round fitness program that uses movement patterns similar to snow-sliding sports may be a solution to this dilemma.

The exercises in these programs become even more effective if you make use of a technique used by professional athletes: visualization. As you perform the exercises in this book, try to develop an image in your mind's eye of how the perfect performance of your sport should look or feel. Some of us call this Skiing or Riding in the Theater of Your Mind. You may even want to perform these exercises while watching a skiing or snowboarding video. Of course, the greater the resemblance of an exercise to a particular snow sport, the easier it is to imagine yourself on the slopes.

Snow-sport fitness is dependent upon two major factors: Deep core muscle activation and neuromuscular coordination. Unfortunately, these aspects of fitness may decline after the age of forty. This can even occur in people who have been fit and athletic for most of their lives. The core musculature has a strong influence on balance, proprioception and centering. As people approach their middle years, these physical factors have their psychological counterparts.

- **Balance** relates to balancing one's lifestyle between work, family, friendship and recreation.

- **Proprioception** is an awareness of where the body is in space. Mental proprioception is an awareness of where you are in your life.

- **Centering** is the result of being at peace with the two factors above.

Baby boomers are not the only ones faced with this juggling act. Those who have attempted to learn a sport as adults might find themselves faced with the challenge of deciphering new, unfamiliar movement patterns.

Children and younger teens keep their "learning muscles" active.

They are constantly exposed to new subjects and new activities. Life is a carnival, with all sorts of amusements to pursue. Then, as we approach adulthood, we tend to specialize our learning in order to focus on what we need to do to earn a living. We bid farewell to the carnival and seek a path that will lead us to the fast track to success. Even high school seniors begin to design their studies in accordance with where they want to go to college and with what subject they would like to choose for their major. Continuing to learn and grow, though, can be challenging at times.

THE STEPDAUGHTER MEETS THE DARK SIDE

When I married Mark, he had two children from his first marriage: Kara, age three; and Greg, age seven. In defiance of stepfamily stereotypes, we got along quite well. But invariably their occasional visits led to some sort of adventure—or, more accurately, a misadventure.

On a whitewater-rafting trip, a bee stung Kara. I fell out of the raft. It rained constantly on a camping trip.

On a hiking trip, Greg fell down the mountain.

We accepted these mishaps with good-natured humor. Obstacles are part of being a good sport, and overcoming them was an inexpensive price to pay for a good time. Adversity need not mean tragedy. Family teamwork can overcome adversity. The stepfamily experience is not always a negative one; the platitudes flowed easily.

One year after I decided that I actually liked skiing, Mark decided to take the family on a ski trip to Whistler. At age fourteen, Kara was already a highly proficient horseback rider. So although the kids live in Florida where, according to Kara, "the garbage mounds are the highest peaks," she took to skiing immediately because of the similarity of skills between the two sports.

On the fifth day of our trip, Mark and Greg were not feeling well, so Kara and I went out together. She wanted to ski down from the top of Blackcomb Mountain. I was amazed that she felt confident enough to do that with only a minimal amount of lessons, but I knew a flat cat track—a narrow trail without any significant amount of pitch—went from the top to the bottom.

I should have been suspicious about the short lift line. Unfortunately, we hadn't listened to the weather reports. We descended from the lift into a complete whiteout, with no visibility whatsoever. The heavily falling snow formed intricate patterns of ice on our goggles. Viewing the terrain ahead of us was like looking into a kaleidoscope.

I had planned to take Kara down the cat track that descends around the more challenging trails. But cat tracks are notoriously narrow. Having skied Blackcomb the day before, we knew that the intermediate trails were quite wide, albeit slightly bumpy. Since we were the only two fools on this part of the mountain, we didn't have to worry about human collisions.

Summoning all our courage, we began our slide into the white abyss. We couldn't see the bumps, so we couldn't plan for them. Fortunately, our innate athleticism allowed us to react with agility to the unseen. The sensation was akin to riding blindfolded on a roller coaster; frightening, yet exhilarating.

Upon reaching the bottom of the mountain, our giddiness drew the attention of everyone in the village. Over dinner, we recounted our tale over and over again. Prior to returning to our condo, I bought Kara a tee shirt that said, "Its hard to be humble when you ski like me."

This was to be the last act of goodwill between us for a long time.

The next day, we all went skiing together. The trails were ridiculously crowded. I've come to realize that crowds instill more fear in me than whiteouts or steep terrain. My skiing becomes defensive, and I revert to beginner skills.

Finishing the trail long after the others left me tense, humiliated, and angry with myself.

I burst into rage when Kara remarked: "Hey, you still snow plow and I don't!"

It's unnecessary to describe my reaction. Suffice it to say that it was inappropriate. I did not see my stepchildren for another two years.

Finally, Mark decided that this had gone on too long. He invited Kara up to Boston for the Christmas holiday. As a peace offering, I bought Kara a copy of *The Centered Rider* by Sally Swift. Looking through it, I realized why Kara was such a natural skier. If you take away the word "horse," everything that Swift says in her book can be applied to skiing.

Kara had become highly proficient at horseback riding. In fact, at age sixteen she had already reached instructor status. But being sixteen meant that she wanted to try the sport that alpine skiers refer to as The Dark Side: Snow Boarding!

Driving out to Sunday River, Maine, I recounted a story to Kara about a ski trip Mark and I had taken the year before. Mark, bless him, has a way of thinking that I am better than I really am. On a trail that was beyond my abilities, I ended up next to an equally terrified ten-year-old boy, who was crying, "My brother is an asshole!"

"My husband is an asshole!" I cried.

The next morning, Kara headed out for her snowboard lesson. Mark and I went skiing. Later, we watched her lesson.

Here comes Kara down the mountain. Boom! She falls. She tries to get up again. Boom! She's down again. This goes on for quite a while.

The next day, she would not let us watch her put her board on.

"Get out of here!" she screamed.

Okay.

Later, Mark asked if she wanted to try to go down a beginner trail. She agreed. But this relatively easy trail was still too challenging.

The goal of the organization Winter Feels Good is to promote the physical, spiritual, and psychological benefits of snow sports. Their website, winterfeelsgood.com, has a plethora of information about how to get started in any snow sport. Although the site is aimed towards parents who want to get their kids involved in a winter sport, it is highly beneficial for anyone interested in skiing, snowboarding, or snowshoeing. At my studio in Frisco, I have found that teenagers who come to class with their parents love the Snow Condition Workout because it is not boring. Why not spend some quality time enjoying this workout with your kids?

Stuck at the trail's edge, she turned to me and said, "I guess my dad *is* an asshole!"

Afterward, she told me that she now understood why I was sensitive about my ski skills. Although she is fit and athletic, she had no natural talent for boarding. It's a blow to the ego if you're considerably coordinated but find something you cannot do well. Both of our self-images revolved around our view of ourselves as athletically capable people. Yet Kara's attitude was considerably more mature than mine. She viewed the escapade with humor and irony. Skiing may be similar to horseback riding, but snowboarding is not.

Since then, I've lightened up. I take minor setbacks less seriously. As a result, I've improved significantly.

There is, believe it or not, a moral to the story. Even if you can't get to the slopes very often, the more you practice movement patterns that are similar to alpine skiing or any other snow sport, the easier it will be to become comfortable at the sport. A surprising side benefit to this newfound proficiency is a confidence to learn other new things. I was totally computer illiterate prior to learning to ski. In fact, I was even afraid to use an ATM machine. I didn't type, so I barely wrote. Then, when I discovered the EpicSki.com ski forum, I started posting messages all day.

SKI TALK: CHATTING ABOUT MY GENERATION

I once had an online conversation with a young female ski instructor who asked whether other young instructors found themselves frustrated with female students who were not raised with Title IX. Although I am not a ski instructor, I felt compelled to reply. I was not raised with Title IX. The women of my generation were cheerleaders, not the athletes themselves. As we grew older, however, and became the early feminists, we fought for the right of the younger generation of females to have equal opportunities for athletic education in the school system.

For this reason, it is often a bit disconcerting for us to be taught be a younger teacher who seems to be bothered by our lack of athleticism. The conversation was very enlightening. While there are many ski instructors cited by ski publications as being the best in the country, many do not have the empathy to work with adult learners. Although this particular instructor was willing to admit to her prejudices and try to understand them, others are not. Later in the book, I will list instructors throughout North America who actually enjoy teaching adult never-evers. For now, however, let's explore the reasons why you might want to learn a snow sport, and the fitness methods you can use to develop the athleticism required for that sport.

When you go to the gym, you obviously have some very specific goals. If you have been working out for years, you have probably discovered that success at obtaining these goals may be rather elusive. As the proverb goes, if you want to make God laugh, tell him your plans. If you want to make him really laugh, tell him about your new weight loss program. Body weight will go up and down like a disobedient child, no matter how hard you try to discipline it. Some muscles just won't tone, no matter how hard you work them.

For some of us, the better we look the worse that we believe we look. This happens because we are using subjective criteria to judge our success. An amusing thing happened when I was trying to find models for the sketches in this book. I approached a beautiful, fit woman in her late forties who I'll call Jeanine. Although she was flattered, she did not think that she attractive enough to be featured as a model. She suggested that I ask another stunning woman, whom I shall call Diana. Diana's response was "Oh no, I'm much too fat! You should ask Jeanine."

If our only reason for working out is vanity, we are bound to be disappointed. On the other hand, developing a fitness plan for enhancing athleticism brings concrete rewards. If you go to the slopes, and do not fall down, there is no doubt that your balance exercises are helping you. If you still feel like skiing at three o'clock in the afternoon, the ski-specific muscular endurance exercises have been worthwhile.

Chris Crowley, co-author of the New York Times bestseller *Younger Next Year*, would probably agree. Chris suggests that we stay young by "climbing out of the ordinary, setting a desperate goal and working like crazy to get there." He also believes in the intrinsic value of the training process itself:

"The training and anticipation perk you up tremendously and give shape and purpose to your daily training." Think about this when you perform the exercises in this book. Concrete goals give us a reason to wake up each morning in anticipation of a brand new day. Just ask my dad.

In March of 2001, my father died, just a few months shy of his ninety-third birthday. He was a man who believed in the perpetual learning process. After he was forced to retire at age sixty-seven, he decided to go back to college. He refused to take special courses for "seniors." Instead, he attended journalism classes at Lehman College, along with the young college students. A few months later, he got a job writing catalogue descriptions for Saks Fifth Avenue. He had always been a good writer. Now he was actually getting paid for it.

After he suffered a stroke, I spoke to him on his deathbed. Although he was not conscious, I told him about Natalie Terry, the seventy-five-year-old ski instructor with whom I had just taken class. He moved a toe in response.

My dad didn't have much money to leave me. Instead, he left me his writing skills, which my passion for skiing ignited. Although I did not have any background in journalism, I began to write about the sport for publications such as *The Professional Skier* and *Aspen Magazine*. Then, before I knew it, I was living this wonderful life in Summit County, Colorado.

Learning a new sport as an adult might take you off the straight and narrow path of what is traditionally defined as success. It does, however, allow you to experience the child-like wonder and excitement that we often lose with "maturity." Life may once again become a carnival that offers you infinite choices for amusement.

Go for it!

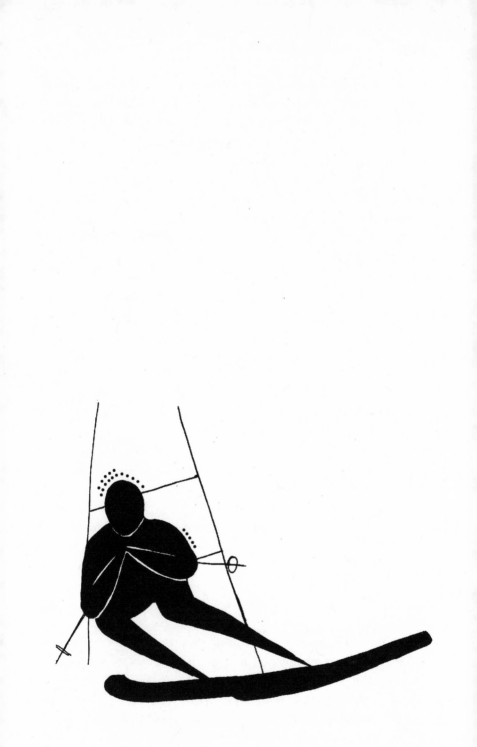

TWO

Embracing Winter

Some like to fly and some like to sail.
Some like the downhill stuff.

—JOHN DENVER

For every sport, there is a season, and a time to train for each and every athletic purpose. To complement these sports, we have been graciously given the gift of four unique seasons. Do you accept these gifts, or do you run from the snow and hide your head in the sandy beaches? All seasons have their beauty. If we are to be truly whole, we should embrace each of them.

While a winter sport may inspire a love for the winter season, these sports present a unique challenge. Why? Because a snowy surface is difficult to replicate in the other three seasons. If you add a bit of imagination, however, to some of the exercises in this book, you can almost feel as if you are playing in the snow.

Although there are a few different types of snow sports, they all have one thing in common. Each winter sport requires you to surrender to gravity and allow the mountain or hill to become your dancing partner. In John Denver's song *Downhill Stuff*, he urges us to keep a-movin' in a forward direction and to let ourselves go with gravity.

With that in mind, it seems fitting that we begin with downhill skiing.

DOWNHILL SKIING

Downhill skiing is also known as alpine skiing. The skis for this sport vary in length and shape, depending on your height, weight and the type of terrain you prefer to ski. In general, downhill skiers use ski poles. The boots are made of reinforced plastic. Bindings keep the boots completely attached to the skis. Telemark skiers, however, use boots that do not attach their heel to the ski. For this reason, telemark skiers are sometimes called "free-heelers."

Very few sports can provide the same sort of thrill, excitement, and challenge you can experience through downhill skiing. While the learning curve might be steep, mastering the required skills is deeply satisfying. Since alpine skiing is my sport of choice, it will be mentioned quite frequently throughout this book. Rest assured, however, that the fitness programs I present are applicable to other snow sports: they all involve a dance with gravity.

CROSS-COUNTRY SKIING

While downhill skiing provides the thrills, cross-country or Nordic skiing provides a great workout. Depending on your weight, the intensity of your skiing, and whether or not you choose to ski hills, cross-country skiing may burn between four hundred and fourteen hundred calories per hour. Since cross-country skiing involves a simultaneous use of the arms and legs, many exercise physiologists consider it to be one of the best forms of aerobic exercise.

The primary difference between cross-country skiing and downhill skiing is that in cross-country skiing, the boot is attached to the ski only with the toe of the boot. The free heel allows cross-country skiers to climb uphill—not very comfortable in alpine skis!

SNOWBOARDING

Snowboarding is a sport that was once the exclusive domain of the younger generation. In the past, it was considered a youth-cult fad. It looks like, however, snowboarding is here to stay. In fact, in recent years, it has begun to gain popularity with the over-forty crowd. Some even claim that it is easier on the knees. Many love the soft, comfy boots, which are a welcome relief from the stiff plastic boots worn by alpine skiers.

Snowboarding involves having both of your feet on one board. Shifting the upper body and hips will swivel the board from its left edge to its right. To stop, you either turn uphill, or deliberately cause yourself to fall by plopping down on your butt.

SNOWSHOEING

Snowshoe enthusiasts tell us, "if you can walk, you can snowshoe." If you have always dreamed of venturing out into the snowy woods without having to learn advanced alpine or Nordic backcountry ski techniques, snowshoeing is the answer to your prayers. On today's short, lightweight snowshoes, anyone can enjoy winter hiking trails just by putting one foot in front of the other.

Snowshoes grip the snow with crampons located at the toe and the heel. This is why you can simply walk along without slipping. Planting the snowshoe flat on the surface enables the crampons to grip the snow and provide stability. Snowshoeing can burn over a thousand calories an hour, making it an excellent form of winter fitness.

GO TELL IT ON THE MOUNTAIN

Participating in a snow sport is a perfect way to conquer the winter doldrums. Snow play, however, is also a great way to explore your relationship with the higher powers. However you define God, the existence of a supreme being becomes evident on the top of a mountain. For some, the spiritual experience comes from the communities that form around snow-sport activities. EpicSki, for example, has over ten thousand members from all parts of the globe.

Others become involved in traditional worship services that are conducted on the mountain. For example, if you are Jewish, you may want to visit Copper Mountain in Colorado and spend a day with the "Adventure Rabbi," Jamie Korngold. Jamie believes that "the spirituality of the wilderness awakens Judaism," and that the mountains allow us to "distance ourselves from politics and protocol and allow the awareness of the connectedness of all things to permeate our souls." She claims, "I am the rabbi who will preach sermons about skiing as easily as I will about Shemini." During the winter season, you can meet Rabbi Korngold at half past twelve on the second Saturday of each month at Solitude Station on Copper Mountain. After a twenty-minute service, the congregation makes some turns down the mountain. For information, visit adventurerabbi.com

For Christians, just about every mountain has some sort of Sunday service. These usually involve a prayer service followed by a group skiing experience. It is, however, important to realize that you don't need to be involved in traditional religious activities to experience spirituality on the slopes.

Sometimes the mountains will simply speak for themselves.

THREE

Core–dination and Snowprioception
(Balance and Awareness for Fitness and Life)

Remember, if you don't do it this year,
you'll be one year older when you do!

—WARREN MILLER

Over the past twenty years, ski enthusiasts have seen evolution-ary changes in both ski and boot design. With these changes in equipment design came changes in ski technique. Brute strength is now less of an issue. The idea that strength should be integrated with balance has taken the spotlight. Sport fitness coaches are beginning to realize that power is compromised if balance and stability are absent. Can you fire a canon from a canoe? Think about it.

With these realizations in mind, the technical focus for skiing has moved from extrinsic control to intrinsic support. Mind/body approaches to technique have become more popular, as evidenced by books such as *Inner Skiing* and *The Centered Skier*.

Meanwhile, the fitness industry has been experiencing similar changes within the same timeline. Mind/body classes have gained popularity. In the sessions of today's fitness conferences, you can hear the echoes of words such as "core," "balance," "stability," and "pro-prioception." These changes in fitness technique and philosophy have been influential in the development of a vast array of training products. Many of these are highly suitable for ski conditioning, especially for adults who find that their balance and proprioception is challenged as they get older. In the ski industry, equipment changes influenced technique. In the fitness industry, technical changes were the impetus for the development of new types of equipment.

Core stability and neuromuscular coordination and proprioception are the most important requirements of alpine skiing and other winter sports. Because of this, I have created the terms "core-dination" and "snowprioception."

These concepts are fundamental to my winter sport fitness program, which I call *Snow Condition* and to which we'll be referring frequently here.

Consider the words of Saint Francis of Assisi: "Start by doing what's necessary; then do what's possible; and suddenly you are doing the impossible." Core-dination and snowprioception are the bare necessities that eventually allow you to do the seemingly impossible in winter sports.

Many people think of themselves as being uncoordinated. Coordination can be defined as the "harmonious functioning of muscles or groups of muscles in the execution of movements." Interestingly, being uncoordinated is defined as "lacking planning, method and organization." To create harmonious movement, the muscles of the body must act in an organized manner. If you were to put the brass section at the front of the orchestra, where the violinists usually sit, you may get a sound that is distorted, that lacks harmony. The same thing happens with the body. If the large muscles take center stage, they will play louder and harder than the muscles that give finesse, grace and harmony to one's movement style.

Contrary to popular belief, being uncoordinated is not a terminal condition! A planned, methodical reorganization of how the body recruits specific muscle groups may eventually teach the body to perform athletic skills in synchronicity and harmony.

If we continue with the musical analogy, proprioception is the ability to know where you are within the score. On the snow, it relates to your awareness of where your body is in space. Proprioception played an important role in Lisa and Kara's Whistler White-out Adventure. Snow conditions challenge proprioception, because they are constantly changing. Thus, I call the ability sense awareness on the snow "snowprioception."

Snowprioception is essential for anyone who wishes to ski or ride in powder. In her book *Deep Powder Snow*, Dolores Lachapelle has this to say:

"Some people can never learn to ski powder snow without exerting tremendous effort and strength because they allow their rational, left-brain hemisphere to control the entire situation." She continues to say that, "there is no longer *me* and *snow* and *mountain*, but a continuous flowing interaction. I cannot tell where my actions end and the snow takes over."

There's no better definition of snowprioception.

Snowprioception is closely related to balance, also a fundamental aspect of core-dination. For this reason, Warren Witherell's *The Athletic Skier* was one of the books that most influenced my philosophy of winter fitness. Witherell believes that there are ten crucial qualities that would qualify a skier to be described as athletic. Although he writes about skiers, these qualities can be attributed to all athletic snow sliders.

First and foremost is *balance*. Witherell believes that the other nine qualities cannot be obtained without "perfect balance."

Let's look at the other nine qualities:

DYNAMIC MOVEMENT

Linked ski turns should be "continuous, integrated and active." Many people ski or snowboard with their legs in a fixed position, which is either perpetually flexed or perpetually straight. If they ski, their ski poles are held out in front of them with their arms in a stiff position. At the end of each turn, there seems to be a pause before the next turn begins. The Snow Condition program incorporates full range movement patterns, while training the transitional balance between movements.

CARVING SKILLS

Skiing requires dynamic use of the feet and ankles. Witherell believes that skiers with poor balance use reactionary balance adjustments, such as thrusting the hands forward. Athletic skiers use anticipatory balance movements, such as edging the skis. The Snow Condition program integrates foot and ankle movements with traditional strength training exercises. As such, it enhances proprioception, which in turn makes anticipatory balance instinctual.

LATERAL MOVEMENT

Athletic skiers are able to execute turns with their feet way over to one side of their body. Have you ever watched Bodie Miller? It sometimes looks as if his ear is in the snow! Lateral movement, often absent in traditional exercise programs, is an important feature of the Snow Condition program. Training lateral movement skills also helps enhance your righting and tilting reflexes. Your righting reflexes help bring your head into the correct position when you are balancing on a non-moving surface, such as standing in a lift line. Tilting or equilibrium reactions generally involve the entire body, and are engaged when you are on a moving surface. For example, if you ride the trolleys in Boston, don't hold the pole when the trolley takes off to develop your tilting reflexes.

STRENGTH

When integrated with balance conditioning, functional, dynamic strength training enhances athleticism in skiers. The Snow Condition program focuses on strengthening the muscles that are specific to snow sports, while maintaining the correct strength ratios between muscle groups.

QUICKNESS AND AGILITY

These two qualities distinguish an exciting snow slider from a boring one. Balance and postural alignment, though, are a prerequisite for practicing agility drills.

ECONOMY OF MOTION

According to Witherell, "Muscles that are busy doing one task are less efficient at doing others." Correcting muscular imbalance promotes movement efficiency.

RELAXATION

Witherell tells us that an upright alignment or "a proud position, contributes significantly to relaxation-allowing muscles to rest and bones to carry weight."

NATURAL, UNAFFECTED STYLE

He stresses spontaneity as opposed to "correct positions." Because of the dynamic nature of winter sports, holding "postures" is ineffective for any type of winter fitness training.

PLAYFULNESS

Witherell urges us to "be delicate one moment and powerful the next" and to "laugh often." Throughout this book, I may sound very serious when I start talking about the benefits of some of the exercises. The element of play, however, should always be present throughout your workout.

Now that you are gaining an understanding of the fundamental requirements for snow-sliding proficiency, you probably realize that your gym workout may not be functional in terms of helping you develop these skills. Keep in mind that I am definitely not negating the value of traditional weight training or aerobic exercise. I still perform these activities on a regular basis. Nonetheless, these exercise forms are predictable, and thus do very little to prepare you for the spontaneity needed for winter sports.

Enough lecturing. Let's talk about the core requirements for fluid, efficient skiing or snowboarding.

CUTTING TO THE CORE

If you were to ask most people the definition of "core muscles," they would answer, "my abs." They are actually, however, referring to the superficial layer of abdominal muscle known as the *rectus abdominus,* the muscles commonly used in traditional abdominal crunches. Training these superficial muscles will help you look great in a bathing suit. There's nothing wrong with that. They are not, however, considered part of the core, and will therefore do very little to assist with balance.

The *rectus abdominus* is associated with spinal flexion, the action performed in abdominal crunches. Ironically, it is designed to be a "fast twitch muscle," which means that it is supposed to be used for quick bursts of activity. Unfortunately, after sitting hunched at a computer in the day, only to rush to the gym to perform hundreds of crunches, many folks have trained their superficial abdominals to become "slow twitch" or endurance muscles. This can explain the hunched posture of many people who seem to be going through a de-evolutionary process in their postural alignment. Performing too many crunches shortens the *rectus abdominus.* As this muscle shortens, it pulls the chest downward. The head and shoulders are pulled forward. The image that comes to mind is of Quasimodo walking through the streets of Paris crying "Esmeralda!"

On the slopes, this postural misalignment can result in loss of balance and sloppy pole technique. This might explain why the king and queen of crunches at the gym become the wipe-out champions on the slopes.

Ironically, our deeper core musculature is designed as a slow-twitch muscle group that will keep us in correct alignment, which in turn has a direct influence on dynamic balance. Since the *rectus abdominus* muscles, however, have been doing their job, they have allowed themselves to become slackers. In fact, they may be so inactive that you might not know where the heck they are hiding. Let's go find them.

The core muscles are embedded deep within your torso. They extend from your pelvis all the way up to your neck and shoulders.

The following structures comprise your core musculature:

- *Multifidus*—A deep muscle running from the neck to the lumbar spine. About two-thirds of your lumbar support is produced through contraction of the *multifidus* muscle.

- *Interspinales, intertransversari,* and *rotatores*—These structures connect to the spinal column. They are important for rotary movement and lateral stabilization.

- Internal/external obliques and *transversus abdominus*—The compressive force exerted by these muscles creates the intra-abdominal pressure necessary for spinal stability.

- *Erector spinae*—These muscles help to balance all the forces involved in spinal flexion.

- *Quadratus lumborum*—This muscle is responsible for stabilizing the twelfth rib during respiration and lateral flexion of the trunk.

- *Transverse Abdominal Muscle*—The transverse is the deepest of the six abdominal muscles. It extends between the ribs and the hips and wraps around the center of the trunk from front to back. Its fibers run horizontally in the same way a back support belt would be worn. Therefore, training your transverse abdominal muscle might eliminate your need for a weight-training belt.

Unless you want to sound impressive at cocktail parties, you do not need to memorize the names of these muscle groups and their actions. A general understanding of their function, though, will help you understand the key elements of snow-sport fitness.

TRANSVERSE LOGIC

Physiotherapist Paul Hodges, Ph.D., can take some of the credit for the current interest in the transverse abdominal muscle. His cutting-edge research, performed at the University of Queensland, explored the relationship between the transverse abdominal muscle and lower-back pain.

It is the function of the transverse to activate prior to all movement, as a means of providing stability. Muscle tests performed by Hodges showed that individuals without lower back pain will contract their transverse abdominal muscle *before* using the muscles needed for movement. People who have back pain will contract the transverse *after* the other muscles, thus compromising spinal stability.

The pelvic floor muscles are also deep stabilizers, and are innervated by the same blood supply as the transverse. Nowadays it's becoming commonplace, and not embarrassing, for fitness instructors to talk about using the pelvic floor in relationship to core stability. The word Kegel (the name of the physician responsible for inventing the pelvic floor exercise) is now so common that it's actually used as a verb.

Although people traditionally describe pelvic floor activation as the feeling of trying to stop the urine flow, you can locate it immediately if you simply cough. Try it. I like to think of the pelvic floor as a hammock being drawn upward. In fact, whenever I get off a lift with a new female skier, I tell her to use this image as she rises from the chair. Miraculously, she gets up smoothly (and, thankfully, avoids knocking me over).

Okay, I know what you're thinking and its just begging to be said, so I will say it for you. Practicing Kegels is also great for your *après* ski life, if you get my drift. Now that is out of the way, so we can move on.

EAST MEETS WEST

For centuries, eastern exercise and martial arts forms have focused on the concept of the center. In modern times, western scientists have shown that there is not only a spiritual but also an *anatomical* basis for this philosophy.

A few years ago, I participated in a ski clinic at the Brighton Ski Resort in Utah organized by the forum participants of EpicSki.com. I was the academy's fitness coach. Our group was blessed with a wonderful ski coach. Weems Westfeldt was Aspen's ski school director and the author of *Brilliant Skiing*. Weems has worked closely with Thomas Crum, Aikido practitioner, and author of the book *Journey to Center*.

Throughout the four days of the academy, Weems put the centering exercises he learned from Crum to good use. Our group consisted of three women; two from the Midwest, and me, at the time a New Englander. We were the lowest-level skiers in the academy, each of us rather timid in our own way.

Although Utah was experiencing an unusually warm winter, there were a few brief snowstorms during the academy. As a result, we were "treated" to constantly changing conditions, which proved to be a challenge to our snowprioception.

Finding your center and then re-centering are important elements in Weems' teaching style. For us, it was the key that unlocked the door to extreme fun as well as major improvement. By day four, we had all increased our speed. We were no longer afraid to be facing directly down the fall line, and we were cutting it up on some of the same trails as the more advanced students.

I recently formed a cyber-friendship with Nicola Speiss, a former Austrian World Cup ski racer. Nicola has had training in the Feldenkrais Awareness Through Movement technique, a system that strives to supplement faulty movement patterns with sequences promoting movement efficiency. Nicola has some interesting observations about skiers who work from a centered position and skiers who have no awareness of center. To paraphrase Nicola, the centered snow-sport enthusiast seems to be saying, "I am a body that functions," while the uncentered snow-sport participant is saying, "I have a body which I operate like a machine."

Centered skiers and snowboarders find that the movements of their sport originate from their center and extend to the peripheral muscles of the body. The movements become integrated with the athlete's entire being, and therefore seem natural. Since these movements are intrinsically controlled, there is no significant need for excessive muscular tension.

In contrast, athletes who are working from an uncentered position originate their movements from the peripheral musculature. Since these movements are extrinsically controlled, they are not as stable, and thus require more muscular tension.

This awareness of center is what is unfortunately missing from some of the so-called core stability exercise programs. In other words, the exercises in this book should not be performed mindlessly. Prior to each exercise, find your center, approximately one-and-a-half to two inches below your navel. There is a definite subtlety to the functioning of the transverse, especially in skiing. For this reason, centering exercises should become a part of daily life. Some Canadian physical therapists have their patients draw the deep abdominal muscle upward and inward for ten seconds, ten times a day. This creates both a more constant awareness, as well as an activation of these muscles. A side benefit is that, for some, it has better cosmetic benefits than crunches.

Developing basic core stability and proprioception skills are crucial before you attempt any of the more challenging exercises in this book. It is quite easy to fake the movements by bracing externally as opposed to supporting the movement intrinsically. On the ski slopes, braced movement can lead to static skiing. Bracing implies rigidity, which is counterproductive to ski technique. Centering is a more useful skill. So while core activation is crucial for proper execution of these exercises, it is not necessary to contract so deeply that referred tension occurs in the rest of the body.

In life, when we are centered, we are able to move in balance without excessive stress and control. The same applies to skiing.

BREATHING LESSONS: THE KEY TO THE CORE

You will notice that breathing patterns are added to many of the exercises in this book. The best snow-sport instructors often incorporate breathing patterns with ski movements, so this gives you a chance to practice them all year round. Additionally, breathing is an excellent way to locate your deep core muscles.

Most people find it easier to engage their transverse abdominal muscle when exhaling. Upon exhalation, the transverse abdominal muscles must compress the diaphragm to expel the air, making it easier to draw the belly in.

Think of the stability ball. If I wanted to flatten the ball, I'd pull out the plug and take out the air. Researchers have also discovered an interesting connection between anxiety and dysfunctional breathing.

Here is an interesting side note about anxiety: In March, 2002, *Outside* magazine published a fascinating article called "At Home in the Discomfort Zone," which discussed the physiology of fear, anxiety, pain and fatigue. In fear-inducing situations, neurons relay impulses from your eyes to your brain, which in turn sets off an alarm to your hypothalamus.

As a result, the adrenal glands pump cortisol, norepinephrine and epinephrine. These stress hormones increase glucose production and heart rate, while speeding up your breathing. The good news is that these reactions turbo-charge your muscles, creating a fight-or-flight response that is actually beneficial to performance.

Researchers have found that anxiety has a different brain circuitry from fear. Anxiety can be described as future-oriented, with a concern for *potential* threats. Anxiety produces a lower level of arousal, characterized by stiff muscles and increased pain sensitivity.

Here's the point I find really interesting: Anxiety stimulates cortisol, but not a significant amount of adrenaline. As a result, the athlete feels paralyzed, and flow state is interrupted. Have you ever observed a person caught at the edge of the trail, afraid to make the first turn? Have you ever *been* that person? Read on!

Fatigue can complicate matters even more. Studies have found that fatigue can not only cause you to lose concentration, it can make you more susceptible to negative thoughts. Since mood drives metabolism, as you become more stressed out, your metabolic rate increases, which depletes your energy stores even more. It takes a good deal of effort the hold the muscles around your neck and shoulders in a contracted position. This waste of energy can lead to fatigue. Adopting a correct pattern of breathing can be helpful in alleviating anxiety and fatigue. Here are some of the dysfunctional patterns. Do you recognize any of them?

- **Hyperventilation:** Do you breathe in a rapid shallow pattern that causes the upper body to tense?

- **Clavicular:** Do you breathe with your mouth open? Since the chest and shoulders rise dramatically with this form of respiration, it consumes more oxygen than it provides to the muscles. This, in turn, can lead to fatigue.

- **Paradoxical:** When you were little, did Mom tell you to take a deep breath and pull your belly in? Unfortunately, Mom was wrong. The deep core muscles function to compress the diaphragm during exhalation. If you are breathing in this manner, the core muscles are disengaged. As a result, balance is compromised.

- **Hypoxic:** You take a deep breath in and do not let it out until the exertion is over. You can get a clear visual image of how much tension this can produce.

While this little lecture may seem like a roundabout way to discuss the importance of breathing, I feel that it's a lesson well learned. On most of the exercises, I will have you inhale in preparation. In general, you will breathe out, or exhale, during exertion. As you exhale, imagine that your navel is pressing toward your spine to flatten the belly. Once you get proficient at the breathing patterns, you can practice engaging your pelvic floor on the return phase of the movement. Remember the image of stopping the urine flow? That describes the biomechanics of how the pelvic floor works. When you are exercising, however, imagine that the pelvic floor muscles are drawing up like a hammock. This will provide extra stability in the return phase of the movement.

Begin the Snow Condition program by practicing the exercises in chapter eighteen, which I call core-essentials. When you have gained proficiency, you can move on to the more challenging program. As you perform each of the core-essentials, as well as the more challenging exercises, think of your belly button as the ignition button that empowers the movements. "Pressing the button" inward toward your spine creates both the energy and stability required to perform the movement in excellent form.

A word about the fear of falling. I once had a ski instructor say that there are two words you should never tell yourself on the slopes: "Don't fall." The brain does not have a visual image for the word "don't." All the brain sees is "fall." Guess what? Boom! Down you go! Instead, as you practice any balance exercise, say to yourself, "Stand up!"

Even when you become proficient in performing the core-essential exercises, you might want to make them part of your daily routine. Exercising your physical balance and proprioception are great ways to reconnect and regain your emotional equilibrium on those days when you feel a bit disconnected from the world.

Hopefully this chapter has enticed a deeper interest in how your body works as an integrated unit. While the next chapter is a bit technical, I have tried to demystify some of the typical "geek talk" associated with the subject matter. Understanding how the chain of events that takes place in any movement pattern is intrinsically related to that specific movement skill empowers you to make better choices when determining exercises for your winter fitness workout.

Thus, without further ado, allow me to introduce you to the kinetic chain.

FOUR

What the Heck is the Kinetic Chain? (And Why Should I Care?)

Fall seven times: Stand up eight.

—JAPANESE PROVERB

I hereby promise that this will be the only chapter where I will resort to techno-babble. Although this subject matter may be a bit complex, it will shed some light on how movements are actually learned. Once you get the gist of what the kinetic chain is and how it works, you will understand why many of the traditional gym exercises do very little to prepare you for snow sports.

The best definition of the kinetic chain can be found in *Optimal Performance Training for the Fitness Professional*, written by Michael Clark and Rodney Corn. They define *kinetic* as a force and *chain* as an interconnected system. The kinetic chain is therefore an "interconnected system designed to absorb, distribute and produce forces" throughout the body. Since the kinetic chain is responsible for all human movement, skiers or snowboarders are only as strong as their weakest links. A weak link can delay reaction times and make snow sliders susceptible to injury.

CHAIN REACTIONS

Graceful, fluid, and efficient snow sliding is closely related to how quickly the skier can react to the unexpected stimuli presented by a constantly changing environment. These may include, but are not limited to, rocks, ice, lift towers, and other skiers. In these situations, the skier or snowboarder's reaction time is of paramount importance.

The term "movement time" is used to describe the period between the end of the reaction time and the movement chosen in response to it. Studies in motor learning have shown that enhancing coordination and correcting muscular imbalances can reduce movement time. Both reaction time and movement time are related to the anticipation of a given stimulus. As your proprioceptive skills improve, you will sense the subtle commencement of changes in the environment before they actually happen. Unfortunately, a predictable weight-training machine, such as the leg extension machine, does very little to train your proprioceptive skills.

The agility and spontaneity required for snow sports must involve training the entire kinetic chain, comprised of the muscular, skeletal, and nervous systems. These components work together to produce human movement. Nowadays, sport-conditioning coaches have a mantra: "Train the chain." This means that the best sport fitness programs will be based on movement patterns that mimic the muscle sequencing used in the sport itself.

While we often focus on the individual actions of the muscles themselves, the nervous system is actually in control of our movements.

No one describes this as well as the physiologist Irwin Korr. "The spinal cord is the keyboard on which the brain plays when it calls for activity. But each 'key' in the console sounds not an individual 'tone' such as contraction of a particular group of muscle fibers, but a whole 'symphony' of motion. In other words, built into the cord is a large repertoire of patterns of activity, each involving complex, harmonious, delicately balanced orchestration of the contractions and relaxations of many muscles. The brain thinks in terms of whole motions, not individual muscles. It calls, selectively, for the preprogrammed patterns in the cord and brain stem, modifying them in countless ways and combining them in an infinite variety in still more complex patterns. Each activity is subject to further modulation, refinement, and adjustment by the feedback continually streaming in from the participating muscles, tendons, and joints."

The nervous system has three functions: sensory, integrative, and motor.

1. The **sensory system** senses changes in the environment, such as "Oh, no, ice!" or "Oh, my goodness, moguls!"

2. The **integrative function** analyzes and interprets this information and helps make a decision as to the proper response.

3. The **motor system** then creates a neuromuscular response to the environment, based on information from the integrative and sensory systems. An example would be the way we (hopefully) know how to alter our walking pattern from when we are in street shoes to when we are in ski boots.

Studies in motor learning suggest that the brain recognizes movement patterns better than it recognizes muscular isolation. The dynamic pattern perspective theory states that movements are learned and produced as a result of interactions between many of the body's systems, such as the muscular and skeletal systems. Memories of these movement patterns facilitate what some movement scientists call self-organization. The athlete remembers what is effective, and organizes movement patterns accordingly.

The skeletal system provides a structure for movement and is comprised of bones and joints. Since movement in one joint affects the movement in another, any misalignment of the joints can throw off the entire kinetic chain. Your muscles, based on the feedback from your nervous system, create movement. They are classified as:

• The **agonists**, which are prime movers;

• The **antagonists**, which act in opposition to the agonists.

One of the major foci of the Snow Condition program is the development of a cooperative relationship between the agonists and antagonists. This is important, since muscular imbalances can result in a faulty movement pattern, which in turn can alter the activity throughout the entire kinetic chain.

In some cases, a muscular imbalance can cause you to begin your athletic movement from the wrong part of the kinetic chain. For example, in skiing, it is obviously in the feet. This is why there is so much emphasis on boot fit and alignment. If lack of proprioception and poor boot fit cause a lack of awareness of the actions of the feet, the skier might initiate their turns by tightening their quads. We call this "muscling the turns." The result is not very pretty.

TRAINING THE CHAIN

The most important concept of the kinetic chain is the fact that the primary information comes from the nervous system. How the body reacts to this information needs to come from good instruction, as well as correcting muscle imbalances and misalignments. Extroceptors and proprioceptors are the messengers responsible for transmitting feedback to the nervous system, which in turn influences the kinetic chain's functionality. Extroceptors receive input from outside the body. Proprioceptors receive input from inside. Graceful, fluid snow sliding depends on your ability to synchronize the input from both sources.

Extroceptors

The eyes are the chief extroceptive organs. Their function in snow sports will be explained in the chapter on vision. The ears are also important extroceptive organs. You can get feedback about your skiing by noticing the difference between the sound of carving and the sound of a skidding. The inner ear is equipped with equilibrium receptors. If you tip your head from ear to ear, or turn it from side to side, you will feel how these receptors preserve equilibrium by maintaining a stable head alignment. Structures within the ear transmit information to the brain regarding head position, and speed of head movement. Some skiers have excessive head movements due to inadequate stability or faulty alignment. This can actually lead to disorientation on the slopes.

Proprioceptors

The proprioceptors are responsible for letting us know our position in space. As snow sliders, our sense of proprioception tells us if we are centered on our equipment. It informs us if we've hit an ice patch, or if we've glided over a bump. When balance is threatened, proprioceptors in the feet, hands, muscles and bones alert the nervous system. The brain then instructs the rest of the body about how and when to react to these changes.

Mechanoreceptors

The mechanoreceptors are the sensory cells that provide feedback regarding joint position. Once this information is processed, they assist in choosing the best muscular response.

IT'S ALL IN YOUR HEAD

Different parts of the brain control different types of movement. The cerebellum compares and integrates sensory information with the external environment. It then helps decide what would be the best movement response, regulating force, ensuring muscle balance, and planning the next movement.

The brain stem is responsible for coordination, balance and stabilization, while the basal ganglia control repetitive movement, as well as the velocity, amplitude and direction of that movement. Traditional weight training and running on a treadmill or activities are controlled by the basal ganglia.

Snow sliding requires balance, however, along with the ability to react to the environment and the ability to plan the next move (which, based on ever-changing conditions, may not be the same as the last one). Therefore, the Snow Condition program is comprised of exercises that will challenge your ability to be spontaneous. Perhaps it is the spontaneity of the sport itself that has the power to transform people's lives so completely. Spontaneity is related to agility, the ability to react swiftly without losing balance, coordination and postural alignment.

Perhaps this would be a good time to talk about alignment.

FIVE

Stand Tall, Stand Proud (Posture and Balance)

I believe that for permanent survival, man must balance science with other qualities of life, qualities of body and spirit as well as those of mind - qualities he cannot develop when he lets mechanics and luxury insulate him too greatly from the earth to which he was born.

—CHARLES LINDBERGH

All movements require a structural base in order to generate and absorb force. This is what we call *posture*. Since posture is the point at which movement begins and ends, movements that begin in less-than-optimal posture may have a less-than-optimal ending. On the ski slopes, this may translate into injury.

Although you may be tempted to view posture as being static, it is actually dynamic, constantly adapting to meet the demands placed on it by internal and external forces. Deviation from correct alignment can cause a change in your center of gravity. This will affect both your structural and functional efficiency.

Maintaining balance through all the segments of the body is defined as postural equilibrium. Optimal alignment is essential to our athletic skill and neuromuscular efficiency. When proper length/tension relationships exist in the muscles, the kinetic chain can produce high levels of functional strength, agility and coordination.

On the other hand, gravity is a bit unfriendly to the misaligned body. Being out of alignment can put us at war with the forces of nature.

When we sense our lack of control, our legs become rigid and insensitive to the feedback that the terrain provides for us. Our shoulders and neck tighten, our jaws clench and our heads jut forward. We think that rigidity gives us stability. In this, however, we are misinformed. In the battle of man or woman against mountain, the mountain will win again and again and again.

Unfortunately, the ergonomics of our daily lives set us up for postural disaster. The way we sit, stand, and walk can cause some muscles to become shortened while others are lengthened. Muscular imbalance will affect the ability of the nervous system to communicate with the muscles.

As a result, recruitment patterns, and therefore movement patterns, become altered. Muscles respond by becoming either over- or under-active. Posture and balance are intrinsically related. Efficient athletic posture allows the knees and ankles to be parallel and slightly flexed. Core muscles are active. Ears are over the shoulders, and the eyes are focused straight ahead. This alignment allows us to be receptive to the forces of gravity.

The war is over. Skiing becomes a dance.

Now let's look at the other factors that influence balance.

FACTORS THAT INFLUENCE BALANCE

- Feet not aligned under hips

- Excessive forward flexion at the shoulders or waist

- Head down or forward, thereby reducing visual field

- Joint stiffness

- Uneven rhythm

- Holding breath

- No reference for pressure control along sole of foot due to lack of proprioception

- Limited endurance
- Insufficient strength to stand on one leg
- Abrupt movements

Physiological factors affecting balance

- General level of fitness
- Kinesthetic sense
- Vision
- Vestibular system (inner ear)
- Motor skills and reflexes
- Athletic stance

Extrinsic factors affecting balance

- Improperly fitted boots and inappropriate ski length
- Gravity
- Friction
- Speed
- Obstacles such as trees, people and lift poles
- Terrain irregularities such as ice or moguls
- Weather conditions, such as whiteouts or fog

Psychological factors affecting balance

- Confidence
- Courage
- Adaptability to new experiences
- Commitment to sport
- Anxiety

- Fear

- Expectations

- Peer pressure or pressure from significant other

I find the psychological issues particularly interesting. As a Pilates instructor, I have pretty decent postural alignment. When I am feeling anxious about the terrain, though, you would not believe that I had ever even taken a Pilates class, let alone taught one. My Colorado ski instructor has a very interesting way of dealing with this issue. He sometimes uses techniques borrowed from the theater world: *acting from the inside out*, and *acting from the outside in*.

According to Michael, "Whenever I direct a show or teach an acting class, I find that there are actors who work from the inside out and actors who work from the outside in. An actor working from the inside out may use a particular experience they've had in the past to find the emotion suitable for the role. When actors can't find an emotional catalyst from inside themselves, they may create the physical qualities associated with that particular emotion. That's called acting from the outside in. If I see a skier who is fearful on the slopes, I may be able to make them feel more confident by adjusting their stance."

This can be a very powerful technique if used correctly. By mimicking the body alignment of a highly confident skier, you can "fool yourself as well" as the song "I Whistle a Happy Tune" says.

We've worked on this idea in acting class as well. At first, Michael has us walk across the room using our normal posture and gait. Then, we alter that gait and posture to suit the character we are trying to portray. It is truly amazing to see and feel how this changes your sense of confidence, either for the better or the worse. Consider this: If simply mimicking the posture of a more confident person can make you feel more confident, imagine how you will feel if you retrain your body and mind in order to make that posture become part of your daily alignment.

Caveat: If faulty alignment is caused by serious muscular imbalances, it may take more than mind games to fix it. No worries, though. We have plenty of exercises in Part Two to deal with muscular imbalances.

The core-essential and snowprioception exercises are the prerequisites for the posture improvement program. Review them prior to working on these exercises. If you seriously want to improve, you might consider supplementing this workout with a class that specializes in improving alignment. These may include, but are not limited to, the Feldenkrais Technique, the Alexander Technique, and Pilates.

Many of the exercises featured in this book have evolved from the Pilates technique. Joseph Pilates was himself a sickly child who suffered from asthma, rickets, and rheumatic fever. Determined to live a healthier life, he developed a technique that he called "controllogy." One of the many sports in which he excelled was skiing. If you take a look at some of the basic principles of Pilates, you will find a striking similarity between Pilates technique and the distinguishing characteristics of fluid, efficient snow sliding:

- **Concentration:** Your mind is engaged on the exercises you are performing.

- **Control:** The coordination of mind and body prevents movements from becoming haphazard.

- **Centering:** Pilates was ahead of his time. He referred to the core as the "powerhouse" of all movements.

- **Breathing:** Upon exhalation, the transverse abdominal muscle presses against the diaphragm to expel air. Proper breathing aids in core activation.

- **Postural Alignment:** As explained earlier, optimal alignment promotes optimal skill.

- **Flow:** Continuity of movement is an essential element of Pilates exercise. It is also an important aspect of alpine skiing. Some ski instructors talk about the "finitiation" of a turn. This refers to the seamless transition between the completion of one turn and the initiation of the next.

- **Precision:** Economy of motion facilitates precise movement.

- **Stamina:** When muscles are aligned and balanced, the body can move with efficiency. Energy is not being wasted. Stamina is increases as a result of this movement efficiency.

- **Relaxation:** Relaxation is crucial for fluidity.

Many people view Pilates exercise as the be-all and end-all of fitness. I see it as a means to an end. The principles, as well as the postural alignment, can be applied to any sport or fitness activity.

SIX

Feet and Ankles (The Chain Begins)

You cannot stay on the mountain forever. You have to come down
again. So why bother in the first place? Just this: What is above
knows what is below, but what is below does not know what is
above. One climbs, one sees. One descends, one sees no longer,
but one has seen. There is an art of conducting oneself in the
lower regions by the memory of what one saw higher up.
When one can no longer see, one can at least still know.

—RENÈ DAUMAL, *MONT ANALOGUE*

The three most fundamental skills of skiing are edging, pressure,
and rotary. In skiing, the kinetic chain starts in the feet and
ankles. If they do not function properly, either due to faulty equipment or poor motor control, the movement continuum that follows
up the chain will probably be forced and unstable. The quadriceps
will initiate moves that were supposed to start in the feet. Turns will
be abrupt, lacking in fluidity, what we sometimes call "muscling"
the turn.

Many people tend to clench their toes when they feel themselves
losing their balance. This merely exacerbates the problem. Clenching
the toes narrows your base of support, which in turn will make you
less stable. The feet have an enormous supply of proprioceptors in
them. Clenching the toes compresses the nerves. When a nerve is

compressed, it cannot provide proprioceptive information to the central nervous system. This can wreak havoc on snow-sport technique.

Did you ever notice that if you sprain an ankle, you will repeatedly sprain the same one every so often? Studies have shown that ankle sprains cause a loss of proprioception. So that ankle you sprained last year has no awareness of the fact that you just stepped into a pothole.

In order for ankle strength and stability to occur, the nerve cells within the joint need to be healthy. The nerve cells, or proprioceptors in the ankle, allow the nervous system to assist in the balance needed for skiing. Injured nerve cells, such as those that occur in a sprain must have their neural pathways retrained, in order to recognize the position of the joint in space.

Here's the problem. Most of us have not been taught proper biomechanics of the feet. The type of shoe we sometimes wear for the sake of vanity compounds the problem.

Re-educating the feet and ankles to work in more functional manner is quite a task, but well worth it in the long run for snow-sport skills *and* for good health. If you are a typical gym rat like I am, the idea of working your feet might at first be somewhat unappealing. After all, foot and ankle exercises won't give you a tighter butt or a smaller waistline, so what good are they?

Foot and ankle exercises are actually more beneficial than you might realize. When your feet regain their natural functionality, your everyday movements become more agile and sensual. This means that you become more efficient when you go running or perform other aerobic exercises. Having functional feet also improves your posture, which in turn improves your entire appearance, as well as your sense of well-being. Exercising your feet and ankles can also give you a feeling of being grounded. Try them when you feel that you need to get your feet back on the ground.

SEVEN

Dynamic Discs and Getting on the Ball

Life should not be a journey to the grave with the intention
of arriving safely in a pretty and well-preserved body, but rather
to skid in broadside, thoroughly used up, totally worn out,
and loudly proclaiming, "Wow, what a ride!"

—ANONYMOUS

Quick! What are the three important skills of alpine skiing? Gold stars to anyone who answered edging, pressure, and rotary. In Part Two, we cover different exercises to help you with your balance before you hit the snow. Two inexpensive types of sport training equipment are used for these exercises: the Dyna-Disc and the rotating disc.

DYNA-DISCS

The Dyna-Disc is about fourteen inches in diameter. One side of the disc is smooth, while the other has protuberances (similar to what you might see on Dr. Scholl sandals). Its cushy surface can mimic some of the worst ski conditions. Dyna-Discs are perfect for practicing your edging skills. If you are on a slippery surface, the protuberances should face downward. For an added challenge to the nervous system, perform the exercises without shoes. Keep your deep core muscles engaged and the body in correct alignment. Practice some of the exercises on a stable surface prior to attempting them on the Dyna-Disc. Part Two contains numerous illustrations of this and other equipment discussed in this chapter and elsewhere in Part One.

ROTATING DISCS

Rotary skills are important for steering. They are also crucial for anyone who would like to learn to ski moguls. The rotary disc is an excellent tool for developing your rotary skills. Although they can be purchased from physical therapy supply stores, discount stores, such as Marshall's and TJ Maxx, often sell a so-called "waist trimming" device called the Twister. They are pretty inexpensive, so it is worth it to buy two of them. The trick to working with the rotating discs is to rotate your feet without moving your hips or upper body.

Dyna-Discs and rotary discs are just two types of fitness equipment that can put the word "fun" into functional fitness. You need not confine your balance training, though, to an indoor fitness routine. You can also develop dynamic feet by going to the park and playing a game of hopscotch, or stepping over the stones of a mountain stream. When you allow your feet to have some fun, the rest of your body can't help but join in.

THE STABILITY BALL

The stability ball is probably one of the most economic and versatile conditioning "toys" you can buy. As I mentioned in the introduction, stability ball exercise was the key to conquering *my* inner klutz. If it were not for the ball, I probably would not be skiing, and I would not be writing this book. One of the many great things about the stability ball is that its rolling movements are somewhat similar to the gliding actions of skiing. Additionally, the ball provides an excellent feedback system. If you are not in correct alignment, the ball will not move in a straight line. With that in mind, three cheers for the ball!

The stability ball dates back to 1963, when an Italian toy manufacturer began making toys using vinyl instead of rubber. Eventually, the balls were used throughout Europe in rehabilitative settings, for orthopedic clients, as well as stroke victims. In 1966, Dr. Elspeth Kong used the balls to develop a ski program for disabled children.

Joanne Posner Mayer, an American physical therapist who studied with Dr. Kong in Switzerland, wrote the definitive book about stability ball training. In 1990, she founded Ball Dynamics International in Colorado. Lindsay Zappola, a physical therapist/Pilates instructor, began to work for her. Lindsay has used the balls in her work with the U.S. ski team.

Ball Dynamics, Resist-a-Ball and the Paul Chek Institute are the three organizations that influenced the use of the balls in a fitness setting.

An article published in the June 2000 issue of Physical Therapy cited an experiment done at the University of Waterloo that used electrodes to test the effectiveness of various abdominal exercises. Isometric contractions were performed on:

- A flat table with knees bent

- A wobble board

- A seventy-centimeter gym ball, with feet on a bench at the same height as the ball

- On the same ball with feet on the floor

The findings were quite impressive. On the curl-ups performed on uneven surfaces such as the ball or wobble board, the muscular contractions of both the obliques and the *rectus abdominus* nearly doubled. The curl-ups done on the ball with the feet on the floor quadrupled external oblique activity.

The authors of the study believe that unstable surfaces create the need for more stabilization of the spine, which is a function of the obliques. Modern skiing requires a good deal of the use of the obliques as stabilizers, as opposed to the counter-rotation of the torso involved in older methods. Training to use the obliques as stabilizers is then a highly functional method of ski conditioning.

Most balls come with a small pump, which means that you can deflate the ball and take it with you on ski trips. I would advise spending the few extra bucks to purchase one of the burst-proof balls, especially if you have pets, children, or both. They have a longer life span, and they do not seem to deflate as quickly as the older models. Below are the standard recommendations for ball sizing:

Ball Diameter	User Height
30 cm. ball (12 inches)	Child or non-sitting exercise
42 cm. ball (17 inches)	Under 5 ft.
55 cm. ball (21 inches)	5 ft. to 5 ft. 7 in.
65 cm. ball (25 inches)	5 ft. 8 in. to 6 ft. 3 in.

GUIDELINES FOR STABILITY BALL TRAINING

• Provide as much unobstructed space as possible.

• Work on a clean floor. Check for sharp objects.

• Avoid wearing loose, baggy clothing.

• When seated on the ball, walk feet at one foot away from the ball.

• Keep feet in alignment with knees.

• Core is engaged throughout the exercise.

There is nothing like a stability ball for adding an element of play to your workout. They seem to invariably inspire an unbelievable amount of creativity in anyone who takes the time to play around with them. I sometimes stop in my tracks when I see some of the cockamamie exercises I see people concocting at the gym. Some of them, though, are actually pretty good, and I've been known to devise what my students consider exercise nightmares on the ball.

Another great thing about the ball is the sense of continuous movement that occurs when you simply allow it to roll. Many ski instructors talk about the idea of "letting things happen" as opposed to "making things happen" on the slopes. When working out on a stability ball, if you let yourself roll with the punches, you will suddenly get a clear understanding of what that means.

EIGHT

The Board Room and the Buzz About Bosu

Even as the sport evolves into different kinds of riders
in different environments, there still seems to be a
common thread that makes us a community.

—PAUL PARKER, TELEMARK SKIER

If you have become bored with traditional workouts, you can add spice to your winter fitness plan by getting on board with balance-board training. There are an infinite variety of balance boards that are used for snow-sport fitness. Some are extremely challenging, such as the Vew-Dew Balance Boards and the wobble boards. Others, like the Reebok Core Board, can be adjusted to make the workout more or less challenging.

Although it is impossible to replicate exactly the movements of skiing or snowboarding on dry land, as you perform these exercises, try to imagine the relationship between the movements you are performing and the ski- or snowboard- specific skill. In some cases, I've provided you with a photograph of a skier or a snowboarder performing moves that bear some resemblance to the specific exercise. If these pictures don't inspire you, however, you can choose another photo, or watch a skiing or snowboarding video as you perform the exercise.

THE REEBOK CORE BOARD

The Core Board is the brilliant invention of Alex McKechnie. As physical therapist to the Canadian World Cup soccer team, the Vancouver Canucks, and the L.A. Lakers, he needed a rehabilitation tool that would present a multi-directional balance challenge to his athletes. The Core Board has unique qualities of recoil and torque. It may twist, tilt, or rotate. But it will always return to its original position. If you move to one side, the board responds with dynamic feedback, by pushing you in the opposite direction.

In 1999, Reebok and The American College of Sports Medicine joined forces with McKechnie to bring the Core Board into the fitness arena. The fact that the board can be adjusted for varying levels of stability made it a viable piece of equipment for stability training in a group setting. The ability to vary the resistance also allows you to work with heavier weights than you would normally use when exercising on a traditional balance board.

> Created in 1954, The American College of Sports Medicine is the largest sport and exercise science organization in the world. They promote and integrate scientific research, education, and practical applications of sports medicine and exercise science in order to enhance people's physical performance, fitness, health, and quality of life.

That being said, Core Boards are somewhat expensive relative to the other equipment discussed here. Additionally, some people find that they do not present a significant challenge to their balance skills. For this reason, most of the exercises in this chapter can also be performed on any traditional balance board.

THE BONGO BOARD

Back in the 1960s, the Bongo board was a popular off-season training device for surfers and skiers. The board has gone through many incarnations throughout the years. It is now a popular conditioning tool for snowboarders. If you look at these two pictures, it's quite easy to understand why.

The Bongo board resembles a skateboard. It has, however, a rotating wheel underneath that allows you to maneuver it in any direction. It is suitable for both indoor and outdoor training. While the grippers on top keep your feet in place, until you become accustomed to the board's movements, you should work with a spotter.

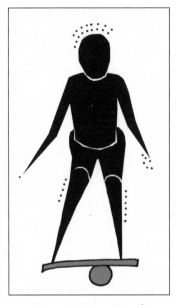

Figure 1: Bongo Board

WOBBLE BOARDS

Figure 2: Snowboarder

The wobble board is another popular snow-sport training tool. Wobble boards are circular and have a sphere underneath that adjusts to your level of skill. Skiers might enjoy working on the double wobble board, which has two platforms located fourteen inches apart. The platforms offer 360-degree rotation and a 22-degree tilt angle.

Aside from being a great balance tool, wobble boards can also help enhance ankle mobility. You can use them while sitting at your desk. Simply place the board under your feet, and rotate your ankles from front to back, side to side, and in a circular motion.

There is something almost humorous about working on a balance board. I find that they are a direct reflection of my mental state. If I am feeling off-balance, lo and behold, I stand on the board and it will not be very user-friendly. When this happens, though, I can use the balance board for a little bit of attitude adjustment. By simply getting on the board, engaging my breathing and allowing myself to find rather than force my balance, I come away in a better state of mind.

THE BOSU BALL

You've probably seen them at the gym. These blue half-balls resemble an elephant's diaphragm. So what's the buzz on Bosu? Continue on!

As the quintessential all-round athlete, David Weck was always looking for a way to improve his balance. Like many cutting-edge personal trainers, Weck believed that balance is the foundation upon which other athletic skills are built. For a while, his training tool of choice was the Swiss ball. But as his skill progressed, he found that the more challenging Swiss ball exercises created a safety hazard.

According to Weck, "While the Swiss ball is a marvelous training tool, its inherent shortcoming is that as you challenge yourself beyond your current capabilities, which you must do in order to progress, the risks very quickly begin to outweigh the rewards. The very exercises that will challenge you are, by the very nature of the ball, increasingly risky, and, ultimately, downright dangerous."

Indeed, there have been far too many incidences of anterior cruciate ligament (ACL) tears incurred by people who tried to stand on a Swiss ball. Besides, if you participate in snow sports, you are more likely to encounter terrain that looks like the mogul-shaped Bosu than you are to be skiing down something that is ball-shaped. Weck created the Bosu to have a training tool that imposed unlimited challenges while staying within the parameters of safety. Bosu means

The ACL, or Anterior Cruciate Ligament, connects near the front of your shinbone. It controls the movement of your lower leg bone in a number of ways. It limits the side-to-side rotation of your lower leg and prevents the shinbone from moving too far forward in relation to the knee. Additionally, the ACL keeps your knee from extending beyond its normal range of motion, as well as providing front-to-back stability. We'll come back to the ACL several more times in this book.

"both sides up." It can be used with either the platform or the dome side facing up.

Weck has some other interesting observations about Bosu training. Many successful, cutting-edge Silicon Valley companies, such as Apple Computers, keep a number of Bosu balls in their buildings. He believes this is due to the fact that exercising on the Bosu "stimulates creativity because it forces your mind and body to work together harmoniously in unpredictable and ever changing ways."

Aside from being an excellent tool for developing snow-sport agility, the Bosu helps develop the mental agility needed for the sport of life.

Professional athletic coaches quickly adapted the Bosu as a training tool. Andy Walshe, Director of Sport Science for the U.S. ski team, considers the Bosu an "invaluable tool" for the U.S. ski and snowboard team. If it's good enough for them, it's good enough for us.

NINE

Jump on the Bandwagon and Slide for the Glide

The five S's of sports training are: stamina, speed, strength,
skill, and spirit; but the greatest of these is spirit.

—KEN DOHERTY

There are three major benefits to using elastic resistance equipment for your ski fitness workouts:

1. **Portability:** Even the most over-packed ski bag can spare some room for a band or two.

2. **Affordability:** If you have spent all your money on equipment and ski vacations, a gym membership may not be affordable.

3. **Variety:** Although elastic equipment may not provide the same strength benefits that weight-training equipment supplies, it is not without its own merits. Bands and tubes provide resistance in both the eccentric and concentric phases of the movements. The concentric phase of a muscular contraction occurs when a muscle is shortening. In the eccentric phase, your muscles are lengthening. Training the muscles eccentrically can be an effective way to prevent injuries.

Resistance tubes and bands provide multi-directional resistance. Most weight-training equipment, with the exception of cable systems, provides resistance in a linear fashion. This isn't how the body functions in sport.

There are two main types of rubber resistance products:

1. **Tubes:** Like all elastic products, exercise tubes come in varying degrees of resistance. Be sure to purchase the door attachments, since they will be useful for many of the "ski-ready" exercises. Resistance tubes come with handles on both ends. This is important for anyone with carpal tunnel syndrome or any other hand injury.

2. **Bands:** Circular-shaped bands can be used for various leg exercises. Therabands are thicker than tubes. Although they usually come without handles, some companies manufacture specific theraband handles. Therabands are popular for post-rehab exercise. We also use therabands for the foot and ankle exercises.

If your time or economical budget does not allow you to join a gym, resistance bands are a perfect option.

SLIDE BOARDS

Once upon a time—over a hundred years ago, actually—a couple of European speed skaters decided to take a barn door, nail slats of wood on either side, and wax the surface, just so they could slide back and forth to train for their sport. A century later, in the latter half of the twentieth century, the slide board experienced a rebirth. Although slide boards did not become very popular in the group exercise scene, they are excellent ski-conditioning tools. Their primary benefit is obvious. The slide board is one of the few pieces of exercise equipment that can simulate the gliding action of skiing.

The slide board itself has evolved significantly from its early days as a barn door. Some athletic gear companies sell a five-foot-long board. The most popular model, though, is a six-foot-long portable roll-up board made of durable plastic.

Keep in mind that a longer board will provide a more intense workout. Most boards come with a pair of booties that fit over your athletic shoes, but a pair of large wool socks will also be sufficient.

Along with being a great workout, the slide board gives you a chance to explore the gliding sensations that are associated with the various types of snow sliding sports. While these sensations may be frightening at first, once you allow yourself to enjoy them, they can induce feelings of total ecstasy.

An instructor at a Vermont ski area was once assigned to teach two women who were part of the resort's Jamaican housekeeping staff. Not only had these women never been on skis, they had never seen snow, nor had they ever practiced any activity that involved this sliding and gliding sensation. Needless to say, they did not enjoy their first lesson. The instructor wished that the ski school had allowed her to take them out on a sled before putting them on skis. That way, they could get used to the gliding sensation in a less-threatening environment.

A slide board would also serve the same purpose.

TEN

Strong and Centered
(Integrated Fitness
for an Integrated Life)

Be braver in your body or your luck will leave you.

—D.H. LAWRENCE

As research in the field of sports medicine becomes more sophisticated, we in turn need to become more flexible in our thinking about ski fitness. Far too often, people become devotees of only one form of exercise, failing to notice that they have *adapted* to it and are no longer receiving any benefits.

I see this at the gym all the time. It happens every season, in every sport. People sing the benefits of a particular fitness program. Flexing their biceps, standing on stability balls, aligning, defining, chanting their mantras, going through too many pairs of running socks to count, they cry "*This* and only *this* will turn me into the best skier, boarder, marathoner, swimmer, etc." But then we hear the bad news. Tales of torn ACLs and rotator cuffs are heard in the locker rooms, and bemoaned on the Internet. Spinal discs are herniated, ribs are cracked, and bones are broken.

Most of the victims of these unfortunate injuries will swear to you, "Oh, well, you know this is what happens when you push too hard, but hey, no pain, no gain, right?" Or maybe we hear, "My karma turned bad," "I lost my alignment," "my core disengaged," or "I sprained my ankle in a pothole."

Be warned: never, ever, tell these people that something may be amiss in their training programs. We are sometimes more faithful to our workout routines than we are to our significant others. Truth be told, nothing is inherently wrong with any of these programs, with the exception of the fact that they are simply *programs,* as opposed to pathways toward educating the muscles to act in a coordinated, synergistic fashion.

Many people find themselves stuck in one dimension of fitness. For these folks, venturing out into other realms of conditioning is akin to visiting another planet. When you decided to learn a snow sport as an adult, you made the decision to break the pattern of your daily activities. Wouldn't it be logical to break the pattern in your fitness routine?

Today, many fitness programs are described as disciplines. Logic would then imply that the followers of these programs are disciples. Indeed, the fitness industry is not without its self-proclaimed gurus, whose followers embrace the principles of the program as doctrines requiring strict, unyielding adherence. The quest for the best exercise and the set of Absolute Truths that accompany it can only be paralleled by the quest for the Holy Grail.

Snow sliding skills represent an integration of a variety of aspects of fitness. No single exercise technique can fulfill all of these aspects.

My good friend Weems Westfeldt, author of *Brilliant Skiing,* has commented that when people reach a point of skill proficiency in many sports, they need to broaden their focus. Unfortunately this is often when they *narrow* their focus and concentrate on only one aspect of the sport, leading to burnout, injury, or both. Indeed, we seem to be coming into an age of specialization, not just in our fitness preferences, but also in our careers. Yet the question remains: Is the straight-and-narrow path the only road to success? My own experiences tell me that it is not.

Once I began to think outside the box in terms of my fitness routines, I started to think outside the state in terms of my life.

BALANCING ACTS

Now that I have you convinced, you are probably wondering how on earth you will find the time to integrate all these aspects of fitness. It's actually easier than you might think.

Let's begin with one of the most popular aspects of sport-fitness training today: dynamic balance. While there are a multitude of balance devices on the market, simple changes in your regular routine can suffice. For example, if you use aerobic equipment, try it without holding the bars.

Changing your position on the machine can also enhance balance and activate different muscle groups. I've seen footage of the U.S. ski team using the elliptical machine in a tuck position with their backs to the screen. If you enjoy using the treadmill, try it standing sideways at an incline. Step up with the uphill leg, and then bring the downhill leg up to meet it. This will strengthen your abductor and adductors (inner and outer thighs) while enhancing lateral balance. In fact, exercising in different planes of movement is an excellent way to create a versatile workout. By varying your positions, you will also improve your functional flexibility.

THE PLANES, THE PLANES!

The technique known as multi-planar movement is rapidly gaining popularity. Traditional weight training is predominately linear. Many, however, believe that it is not truly functional, since most activities take place in varying planes of motion. If you have been using machines exclusively, try some exercises on the cables, which enable you to use a variety of positions for each muscle group.

Multi-tasking is another way to add new dimensions to your fitness routine. This workout method involves exercising various muscle groups simultaneously. For example, you can perform a lunge with one leg forward, while performing a one-armed row with the opposite arm. Since we never isolate muscle groups in real-life activities, multi-tasking is yet another way to make you workout more functional. There is also an added side benefit: By using more muscle groups at once, you'll be burning more calories than you would by performing traditional strength-training exercises.

INTEGRATED TRAINING

Integrated Training is a technique that was popularized by the National Academy of Sports Medicine. The program, called Optimum Performance Training, consists of seven phases. For the purposes of this book, I will briefly describe four of them.

In the early stages of training, you are working on postural correction, as well as techniques to enhance balance and stability. As the student progresses, traditional weight training exercises are followed by a balance exercise that uses the same muscle group. Once a significant amount of strength, stability and alignment are achieved, one can integrate a traditional strength exercise with a plyometric exercise that uses similar muscle groups.

PLYOMETRICS: JUMP, JUMP, JUMP FOR YOUR LOVE OF SNOW SPORTS

Traditional strength exercises can also precede a plyometric exercise that uses similar muscle groups. Olympic ski teams are currently using plyometric training as a form of injury prevention, as well as a power-training tool. Plyometric exercise incorporates eccentric deceleration, a crucial component of ski technique.

The three major forms of muscular contraction are isometric, concentric and eccentric.

1. **Isometric** contractions do not involve any changes in muscle length. For example, the transverse abdominal muscle activates isometrically to stabilize postural alignment.

2. **Concentric** contractions involve muscle shortening. Ski turns are initiated with concentric contractions.

3. The most important phase for skiers and snowboarders is the **eccentric** phase of contraction. This happens in the last seventy-five percent of a turn. As the quadricep muscle lengthens, the

hamstrings shorten. Gravity exerts an outside force more powerful than the internal forces created by the muscle. This causes the
quadriceps to lengthen, while the hamstrings try to counteract the
movement.

> Some athletic coaches actually use plyometrics as a means of pre-
> venting ACL injuries in female athletes. Since girls tend to land
> from a jump with their knees extended, the ACL is unprotected.
> Plyometrics teaches them to flex their legs upon landing, thus mini-
> mizing the hamstring/quadricep muscular imbalance.

If you like to engage in highly dynamic techniques such as mogul
skiing, there is a rapid interplay between the eccentric and concentric
phases of contraction. Mogul skiing activates what's known as the
stretch reflex. The muscles respond by recoiling dynamically. With
practice, this makes them more powerful. Your muscles are strongest
during the eccentric phase of contraction. When a concentric contraction follows an eccentric contraction, force is significantly increased.
During the eccentric phase, energy is stored in the elastic components of the muscle. If a concentric contraction immediately follows,
this energy becomes available for force production.

Although plyometric exercise is an excellent training tool for skiers, it is not without its contraindications. Needless to say, if you are
injured, plyometrics may not be the best choice. In order to be performed safely and effectively, core stability and postural alignment
must already be intuitive.

You should already have a respected amount of eccentric and
concentric strength, both of which will support proper landing technique. When landing from a plyometric jump, flexion should occur
in the ankle, knee and hip for proper shock absorption. This will
allow you to use the elastic component of the muscles to absorb the
forces of landing, and use them for force production in the dynamic
movement that follows.

The entire foot should be used in landing. If you are only landing on the toes or the heel, the skeleton, as opposed to the muscles, will absorb the shock. This can lead to injury. Flexion should occur in the ankle, knee and hip for proper shock absorption. This will allow you to use the elastic component of the muscles to absorb the forces of landing, and use them for force production in the dynamic movement that follows. Loud slapping noises on landing indicate that the landing technique is incorrect and the exercise should stop.

WHY DOES IT WORK?

The traditional strength-training exercise wakes up motor units in the muscle. The stabilization exercise coaxes the muscle to come out of isolation and play with the other muscles in the body. Meanwhile, the stabilizers, which may have been on a temporary hiatus, are encouraged to play their role in supporting the prime movers. As a result, the body is trained to work in a way that is more specific to sport.

In what NASM calls Elastic Equivalent Training, a traditional strength-training exercise precedes a plyometric activity. The traditional exercise acts as a recruiter, calling large numbers of motor units into action. The resulting synchronization of these units increases force production.

There is great beauty in the inherent logic of this program. Correcting muscle imbalances and providing movement sequences that change the faulty recruitment patterns enhances postural alignment. This in turn facilitates stabilization, the next phase of the program. Since your posture is improved and muscular imbalances are corrected, when you get to the strength-training phase, you have a greater chance of doing the exercises in good form. This hastens the strength-training process. At the final stage of training, you have excellent alignment and stability. You're strong in both your concentric and eccentric phases of contraction, which improves your landing mechanisms for plyometrics.

BENEFITS OF STRENGTH TRAINING

Strength-training exercise causes your muscles and bones to continually renew themselves. Old, degenerated cells and tissue are swept out. New tissue that is stronger and healthier is rebuilt. If the muscles are not challenged by weight-bearing exercises, the body has no impetus to renew itself. This causes tissues to become old and frail, making them susceptible to injury and disease. Strength training can also prevent loss of bone density. This is especially important for women, who may be susceptible to osteoporosis as they get older.

Strength training also increases metabolic rate. One-half pound of muscle loss occurs every year after the age of twenty-five. This produces a one-half percent reduction in basal metabolic rate (BMR) each year. A reduced BMR means that we are less able to use the food we consume as energy. More food becomes stored as body fat. "Basal metabolic rate" refers to the minimum amount of energy used by our body at rest to maintain normal body functions.

Even when we are not engaging in non-athletic activities, we have high energy requirements. While sleeping, our muscles use more than twenty-five percent of our energy (calories). With a well-designed strength-training program, you will achieve an increase in lean muscle mass throughout your body while increasing your BMR. In other words, you will actually be burning more calories in a sedentary state, even in your sleep. Increasing muscle tissue causes an increase in metabolic rate, while decreasing muscle tissue causes a decrease in metabolic rate.

Aside from the benefits I've already mentioned, a well-toned body can work wonders for your self-image. Once you have achieved a certain amount of muscular definition, you may find that you become less obsessed with numbers on the scale. Strength training is also highly beneficial for your sense of confidence. When your body feels strong, you can convince yourself to tackle the most challenging situations that life throws at you.

TYPES OF STRENGTH

- **Starting strength** allows the skier or snowboarder to produce high levels of force at the start of the turn. You can see this sort of strength demonstrated by ski racers at the start of a run. It is dependent upon the athlete's intramuscular and intermuscular coordination. (Intramuscular coordination describes the recruitment and synchronization of motor units within a muscle. Intermuscular coordination is achieved when the stabilizers, agonists, antagonists and synergists work together in integrated movement patterns.) In life, starting strength is experienced by the willingness to take on new challenges.

- **Explosive strength** refers to acceleration. It is the ability to develop a rise in force production after the turn has been initiated. On a personal level, your explosive strength is indicative of the passion you feel when you become involved in an activity you love.

- **Reactive strength** is sometimes called **elastic strength**. The muscles quickly switch from eccentric to concentric contraction. This type of strength is used in plyometric training. Freestyle skiers and snowboarders demonstrate excellent reactive strength. Personal reactive strength relates to your ability to have a swift and powerful response to the curve balls that life throws at you.

- **Endurance strength** describes the ability to maintain force production over a prolonged period of time. Skiers and riders, who enjoy the longer trails at mountains such as Whistler, need endurance strength. In life, when we come upon the more challenging days, our endurance strength helps us get through them.

- **Stabilization strength** refers to the ability of the stabilizers to maintain joint integrity and optimal postural alignment throughout all movements. Our personal stability helps us maintain our personal integrity, while keeping us aligned with reality through all situations in life.

- **Functional strength** refers to the ability of the muscles to work with maximum efficiency throughout all movements. It is related to optimum strength, which describes how much strength is needed for any given movement. In skiing, generating more force than is needed can cause the skis to skid. When we are functionally strong, we have a rational understanding of how to handle life's challenges without being overly forceful.

STRENGTH TRAINING GUIDELINES

The American College of Sports Medicine has the following recommendations for weight training:

- Perform a minimum of 8–10 exercises that work the major muscle groups

- Perform 1–3 sets of 8–12 repetitions

- Weight train 2–3 days a week, with a forty-eight-hour rest period between days. If you are accustomed to doing "split routines" which involve 4–5 weight-training workouts a week, make certain that you are not working the same muscle group two days in a row.

- Exercises should be performed in a controlled manner.

- Use both eccentric and concentric muscle actions.

- Exercise large muscle groups before small muscle groups.

- Perform multi-joint exercises prior to single-joint exercises.

Since you are training for sport performance, good form is important. If the load is too heavy, alignment will be compromised. This can be detrimental to your skiing. Since training is neurological, you may be training the body to respond with faulty recruitment patterns.

In general, use a heavier weight for the traditional exercise and a lighter weight for the stability exercise. Your goal should be to bridge the gap between how much resistance you can use for *both* exercises.

CLOSED-CHAIN VS. OPEN-CHAIN EXERCISES

Strength-training exercises can be classified as either closed- or open-kinetic chain. In closed-kinetic chain exercises, the end of the chain furthest from the body is fixed. An example would be the squat. Your feet are fixed and the rest of the leg chain moves. In open-chain exercise, the end is free, such as in a leg extension machine.

Closed-chain exercises emphasize joint compression, which enhances joint stability.

Open-chain exercises involve shearing forces, which run parallel to the joint.

Closed-chain exercises generally use more than one muscle group. A leg press or a squat will work the quadriceps, hamstrings and gluteals.

Open-chain exercises usually involve muscle isolation. The leg extension works only the quadriceps. Because of the shearing force applied to the joints, many top-level orthopedists and physical therapists advise against this exercise.

There are other factors to consider. The hamstring/quadriceps strength ratio should be approximately sixty to seventy-five percent. In other words, your hamstrings should be sixty to seventy-five percent as strong as your quadriceps. Many people don't even come close to this ideal strength ratio. Quadriceps that are significantly stronger than the hamstrings can lead to faulty ski technique. Additionally, having weak hamstrings can make the skier more susceptible to ACL injury.

Doing extra work that involves quadriceps isolation doesn't seem to make much sense. Since snow sports are, for the most part, closed-kinetic chain activities whose actions initiate in the feet, most of the routines presented in Part Two will consist of closed-chain exercises. These exercises help you feel grounded, as if you have solid legs to stand on.

ELEVEN

The Cat and the Salamander (Agility Training for Life and Sport)

If you keep on doing what you always did,
you'll keep on getting what you always got!

—ANONYMOUS

In any snow sport, the ability to react to environmental changes without losing alignment or stability is an important skill. Chip Richards, a champion freestyle skier, has a lot to say about this. In 1996, he was working with the Australian freestyle team. Although these skiers displayed enormous strength when executing traditional weight-lifting activities, they were also highly prone to injury. Slight changes in snow conditions would throw them off balance.

Then one day he watched his skiers playing soccer. He noticed slow reaction times and only minimal coordination and foot speed. Richards realized that his skiers were unable to harness their gym-acquired strength when executing dynamic movement. They were strong in predictable environments. But they were lacking in their athleticism.

Richards decided to change their conditioning routines and engage in what he called "movement vocabulary expansion." To create more fluidity in his athletes' movements, he had them study Pilates. Additionally, he had them participate in other sports, such as surfboarding and tennis. The following season, the Aussie team received their best results in international competition.

Richards used agility training to improve the skills of his ski team. Agility is the ability to spontaneously react to changes in the environment without losing alignment or dynamic stability. In addition to enhancing athleticism, agility is an important life skill. Think about it. Are you able to react to the mogul fields, icy paths and narrow trails that life throws at you without losing your center? If you were an animal, would you be a cat or a salamander?

The analogy of the cat and the salamander was created by Paul Chek, who pioneered treating the body as a whole system and finding the root cause of a problem. Chek talks about there being two different athletic personality types, cats and salamanders. "Cats" are involved in unpredictable sports, such as basketball and soccer. Some skiers, such as the ones described in Witherell's *Athletic Skier*, can be described in this manner. Cats are characterized by their quick reactions to varying stimuli. When put on a conditioning program, they will respond quickly, and require additions, advancement and variety at frequent intervals. Chek describes the sports they are involved in as being "acyclical." Acyclical sports include hockey, soccer, basketball, football and other sports that require a fast reaction time.

"Salamanders" are slower in their reaction times. They prefer sports such as swimming, weight training and distance running, which in some cases are somewhat more predictable than the activities preferred by cats. Salamanders will take a longer time to adapt to a conditioning program, and are more comfortable repeating the same routine for a longer period of time.

Skiing is interesting in this regard. For the most part, it is a cat-like activity that requires the constant ability to react to changes. Many people, however, take a salamander's approach to the sport. They ski the same trails with the exact same turn shape for each and every turn. While they usually ski safely, if a child, a tree, another skier or a snowboarder finds its way into their path, they may find themselves unable to maintain stability when they react to this unexpected obstruction.

In acting class, Michael tells us acting is reacting. Of course, you can simply read the script and follow the playwright's stage directions, but is that really acting? In the same way, you can ski or snowboard down the same slope each day, while picking the exact same line, moving at only one speed, and using only one turn shape. But does that really allow you to become part of the action? I think not.

Whether you are on the slopes, the stage, or simply enjoying your life, agility training offers you an invitation to come out and play. Use your imagination. Play tag with a child. Chase your dog around the park. Have fun! Agility is a fundamental skill for life. If you can move through each unexpected situation without losing your center, you will allow yourself to take delight in the spontaneity of daily living.

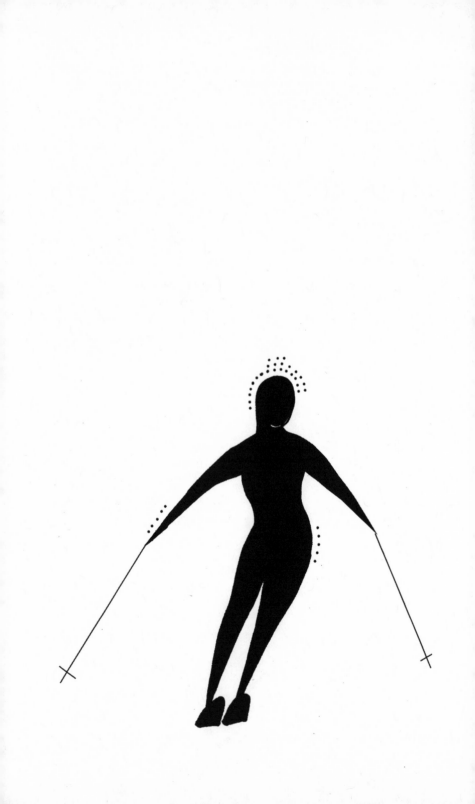

TWELVE

Open Your Heart with Aerobic Fitness

Because, sometimes, merely refusing to stop cultivating an unquenchable lust for beauty and truth and orgasmic life is the most profound and important thing you can resolve to do.

—MARK MORFORD

Okay, let's get ready for the great debate. Why do skiers need aerobic fitness, if they often spend more time waiting for and riding the lifts than they do on the slopes?

As a professional body-shrinker, I will act like a traditional shrink and answer a question with a question. Of all of your friends, who has more energy throughout the course of a day, friends who are aerobically fit or friends who don't participate in aerobic exercise? Enough said. In case you're not convinced, consider this: Aerobic activity increases the body's production of endorphins, considered the "feel good" hormones. When you participate in aerobic activity on a regular basis, it becomes easier to maintain the kind of positive attitude that is capable of counteracting stress.

TRAINING AT THE HEART OF THE MATTER

Cardiovascular training for snow-sport enthusiasts should involve both the aerobic and anaerobic systems. Bump skiers and racers may need a bit more anaerobic training. If you like to ski or ride the seven-mile top-to-bottom trails at Whistler, some extra aerobic training is advised. To determine the difference between aerobic and anaerobic, a basic understanding of heart rate and training zones is helpful.

Recommended training zones are based on a percentage of your maximal heart rate (MHR). The formula for determining MHR has been oversimplified. The standard method is to subtract your age from the number 220. But research has shown that trained athletes may have a higher MHR than sedentary individuals. To further complicate the issue, different training modes will elicit different maximal heart rates. These potential inconsistencies should be factored in, if you are using heart rate to determine your appropriate training zone.

Let's look at training zones:

- **60–70% of MHR:** Energy-Efficient or Recovery Zone: In this zone, you are developing aerobic endurance. If you're doing interval training, return to this zone in your recovery phase, in order to restore the glycogen that was depleted in the anaerobic phase.

- **70–80% of MHR:** Aerobic Zone: In this zone, the cardiovascular system is transporting oxygen to (and carbon dioxide away from) the working muscles.

- **80–90% of MHR:** Anaerobic Zone: This is where you reach your lactate or anaerobic threshold. Glycogen becomes your major energy source. Burning glycogen produces by-products: lactic acid and hydrogen ions.

One hydrogen ion is formulated with each molecule of lactate. The increased concentration of hydrogen ions causes muscle acidity. As a result, nerve endings become irritated, possibly causing pain, nausea or disorientation. Some people find that they reach their lactate threshold at relatively low training intensities. There are a number of reasons for this. Either due to inadequate amounts of oxygen or mitochondria, your heart and muscles may not be efficient at removing lactate from the bloodstream. Lactate threshold training can re-educate the buffering systems in the body, making them more efficient in the removal process.

If you find heart rate monitors or pulse taking too geeky, you may prefer to use the Perceive Exertion Scale. On a scale of 1–20, the following perceived values apply:

6 20% effort—Very, very light (rest)

7 30% effort

8 40% effort

9 50% effort—Very light (gentle walking)

10 55% effort

11 60% effort—Fairly light

12 65% effort—Light

13 70% effort—Moderately hard (steady pace)

14 75% effort

15 80% effort—Hard

16 85% effort

17 90% effort—Very hard

18 95% effort—Harder

19 100% effort—Very, very hard

20 Exhaustion

Research in the *Journal for Sport Science* has suggested a high correlation between rate of perceived exertion and heart rate.

TRAINING PROGRAMS

Take It Outside

When you decided to take up a winter sport, you began an intimate relationship with the great outdoors. Like any other relationship, this should be nourished and maintained all year round. While

there are a number of excellent indoor aerobic activities that can provide indoor training for your winter sport, taking your training outdoors is both physically and spiritually satisfying. In fact, it might be
a good idea to visit the mountains where you practice your winter
sport. The intimate relationship that develops can be amazing. Getting to know the mountain without its layer of snow reveals sub-
tleties and nuances that you didn't know existed.

Even if you cannot get to the mountains, dynamic outdoor aerobic
activities can be beneficial to your winter sport training.

Many skiers enjoy inline skating in the off-season. The International Inline Skating Association now has a Skate-to-Ski summer
course. Check out their Web site at iisa.org. Inline skating works a
number of the same muscle groups that are used in dynamic, athletic
skiing. A skating session works the quadriceps and gluteals, along
with the hip abductors (the outer thighs) and the adductors (the
inner thigh muscles). These muscles work in conjunction with the
quadriceps to support and stabilize the knee joint. In fact, some ski-
ing-related knee injuries can be rehabilitated on skates. Additionally,
the core stability you gain from training on inline skates will transfer
directly to your skiing skills.

There are some interesting parallels between inline skating and
skiing. The essentials skills of balance, edging, pressure, and rotary
motion are crucial components of both sports. Skating throughout
the warmer months can fine-tune your balance. This is because
skates are much shorter than skis. If you compare standing on a
platform that is only 25–30 centimeters long (the average length of
inline skates) versus one that is 145–180 centimeters long (the average length of shaped skis), you will definitely find that it is significantly more challenging to balance on the shorter platform than
on the longer one. This is why some ski instructors teach balance
skills on 99-centimeter snow blades. An excellent ski-specific drill
that addresses balance is gliding on one foot at a time. This can
help you identify the balance discrepancies between the right and
left leg.

Inline skates have edges, just like the ones you see on alpine skis.

Ski-specific skating drills can be practiced on a flat surface or on a slight slope in order to simulate skiing. You can also use a series of cones to simulate slalom gates. If you are an advanced skater or skier, you can practice turn dynamics such as edging and weight transfer. You can even work on the timing and coordination of your pole plant. You can cover your ski pole tips with duct tape or with tennis balls with a hole punched in them. One of the major benefits of ski-specific training on skates is that your turns cannot be skidded. They *must* be carved. This allows you to get some off-season carving practice before you hit the slopes.

Good News For Snowboarders

Thanks to Kurt Tierney, co-creator of the Tierney Board, snowboarders now have an awesome summer cross-training tool. Although the Tierney Board looks like a skateboard, it has some important distinctions that make it suitable for snowboard fitness.

According to Tierney: "With a typical four-wheel board, the more you want it to turn, the harder you have to push on the rail to make the board steer. On the T-Board, with speed, you lean your head and your body and board effortlessly follow."

The two-wheel design of the T-Board makes it one of the few off-season snowboard-training devices that can carve on edge. As it gains speed, its stability actually increases. Here are some things to keep in mind when riding the T-Board:

- **Basic Stance:** Keep in mind that the T-Board is not a skateboard. Your feet should be sideways on the board, not facing front. The board is directional, so make sure you are moving toward the front end of the board. Face down the slope with your legs slightly bent, your shoulders turned forward and arms extended to enhance balance.

- **Turns:** Keep your arms in front for balance. Turns are made with the body, not the feet, by leaning forward or backward and from side to side, toward the toe edge or heel edge of the board for steering and speed control.

- **Slowing/Stopping:** For starters, don't ride beyond your limits. Okay, that said, the best way to reduce your speed is to carve back and forth into the hill in a swooping "s" until you reach a speed with which you're comfortable. The best way to stop is simply, in a controlled manner, to step off of the board.

- **Safety:** All sports carry a risk of injury. Sometimes accidents happen that are truly unavoidable, but usually there are ways to reduce the risks of injury:

  1. Always wear protective gear. This includes helmets and knee, elbow and wrist guards.

  2. Inspect your board before every session. Check the wheels for excessive wear. Make sure all bolts are tight and the wheels are seated properly, and examine the platform for cracks or stress lines.

  3. Live to ride another day. On any new terrain, start slowly. Test the traction limits of your wheels. Carve progressively harder to determine the limits of your comfort zone.

Open Your Heart and Enhance Your Skills with Running

If you are a runner, find a hilly course. On the downhill, run various turn shapes. Cross-country running will enhance ankle proprioception. Since adapting to changes in terrain is an important aspect of skiing, this can be an excellent training tool. Mountain biking is also a great way to maintain your balance skills.

Save it for a Rainy Day

If outdoor training is not feasible due to weather conditions, set up an aerobic circuit in the gym. Ski-specific moves can be performed on the urban rebounder, a mini-trampoline. Jumping rope can promote fast feet and agility. The slide board features lateral gliding movements, which can be beneficial to skiers.

Bosu has an aerobic workout that is similar to a Reebok step workout. The Bosu, however, will provide more of a challenge for ankle proprioception and stability. If you are lucky enough to belong to a gym that uses the Bosu for their group fitness program, you can set up a Bosu Mogul Run. Arrange the bosu in a pattern resembling a mogul field. You can either jump from Bosu to Bosu, or you can jog over and then around them. You can also incorporate some of the agility and plyometric exercise into your circuit. Varying your landing surfaces as much as possible will make your aerobic workouts more ski-specific.

The U.S. ski team does lactate threshold training in the off-season. According to Andy Walshe, their training director, the program trains "your body to burn lactic acid as fuel, allowing you to ski with a burn, but not burn out."

You can measure your own lactate threshold, but do *not* attempt this program without your doctor's approval. You will need a heart rate monitor for this workout.

Take a stationary bike test to find your lactate threshold. The test should take thirty to forty minutes. It's important that you build up gradually, or the test results will be inaccurate. Warm up for ten minutes at zero resistance. Continue at the same pace, but raise the resistance slightly. Pedal for another three minutes, and then take your heart rate. Spin for one more minute, without resistance. For the next three minutes, raise the resistance until your heart rate is higher than the one you took after the first interval. Note your heart rate, and then spin at another minute with low resistance. Continue the rest/interval cycle, gradually increasing the resistance. At around thirty or forty minutes, you will reach a point where both your legs and lungs are burning. You will have a very strong desire to quit. Welcome to your lactate threshold.

You can structure your workouts around your lactate threshold. Use either your heart rate monitor or the Perceived Exertion Scale. The U.S. ski team workout is a five-day-a-week, six-week-pre-season program. Each workout lasts thirty minutes to an hour. Three days a week, you will be exercising in your easy zone, well below your lactate threshold. You should be able to hold a conversation at this pace. On the other two days, you will do a ten-minute warm-up in the easy zone, then you will do three-to-five-minute intervals in the steady zone. Breathing will be labored, and you may find it difficult to conduct a conversation. Each week, increase the length of these intervals until you can stay in the steady zone for ten minutes. In the last two weeks of the program, you can do a few intervals in the hard zone. You will be training when your legs are burning. This will train the body to work efficiently in exhausting snow conditions.

Regardless of which aerobic training mode you choose, be sure to perform the activity in correct postural alignment. This will ensure movement efficiency, which will, in turn, enhance aerobic benefits.

THIRTEEN

Visions of Beautiful Snow-Sliding

Vision without action is a dream.
Action without vision is simply passing the time.
Action with vision is making a positive difference.

—JOEL BARKER

Funk and Wagnall's Standard College Dictionary has two separate meanings for the word "vision":

1. The sense of sight.

2. The ability to anticipate and make provisions for future events.

For most snow sports, vision, in both senses of the word, is a major key to success. For example, if you like to go tree skiing, you know that you should focus on the spaces between the trees, instead of the trees themselves. In other words, if you search for opportunities, you will discover them. If you are looking for obstacles, though, you will surely find them, if they don't find you first. Skiers and snowboarders with *sisu* develop strategy by keeping both their eyes and minds focused on the space between the trees: Sounds like a good plan for life!

Since visual skills are related to strategy, it behooves us to develop

them. The body will go where the eyes are looking. My instructor
proved this to me on a short tree-skiing run. He stood at the exit
from the trees and had me look at him, rather than at the trees. I did-
n't hit the trees. The eyes are the initiators of actions. The body
moves in response to visual cues.

In chapter eleven we discussed agility. You have probably noticed
that agility is directly related to your visual skills, which are sometimes challenged by the glare of the sun and its reflection on the
white snow. In fact, the eyes play a key role in two primary systems
of movement control.

The focal system is involved with the identification of objects. "Is
this a tree or a snowboarder I see before me?" Light has a strong
influence on the functionality of the focal system. You might have
learned this the hard way if you have ever skied in the flat light of
the afternoon. Here's a tip if you end up in that situation. Ski close to
the trees, because the shadows will provide contrasts.

The ambient system controls the central and peripheral visual
field. It perceives movement as well as the position of people and
objects in the environment. "How close is that snowboarder to me?"

The term "optical flow" is used to describe the reflections of light
that pass through your eye from your environment. Optical flow
provides information about your movement within that environment. This includes your stability and balance, the velocity of your
movement, the direction of your movements in relationship to other
skiers in the environment, and the amount of time before you and an
object or another snow-sport enthusiast collide. Perhaps this is why
so many ski accidents occur in the flat light of the late afternoon.

In some cases, postural alignment may have an adverse affect on
vision. This is sometimes the case for skiers who have the classic for-
ward-head alignment. Sometimes vision, though, is responsible for
poor alignment. It is the quintessential chicken or egg question. Your
best solution is to have both your postural alignment and your
vision evaluated.

In the meantime, I'll bet that you never thought that visual training was an important part of your snow-sport fitness program. Yet

consider the visual challenges you face during a typical ski run. Poof! Out of nowhere, a family of seven appears in your path. "Wait a minute, how did that tree get there?" You get the picture? As snow-sport enthusiasts, we need to shift our gaze smoothly and rapidly from points in the distance to points in proximity. The ability to see changes in terrain enables us to plan and react appropriately. It's called *strategy*. Just as in life, you cannot have strategy without vision. About eighty percent of the information we receive is visual. Because of this, when we improve our visual skills, we enhance our motor coordination.

Here's how it works. The eyes send visual information to the brain, which in turn integrates the data and turns it into a three-dimensional image. This process is called fusion. If you are not focusing on something specific, such as a tree, a slalom gate, or another skier, your eyes will take in the entire visual field.

Let's say, however, that there is an incredibly hot ski instructor up ahead of you. If you focus on that person, it is called fixation. A caveat: Studies have shown that the average range of focus is approximately three degrees. Since the focus of the visual field is so small, peripheral vision becomes a crucial aspect of sport vision. Anyone who has ever been side swiped by another snow-sports enthusiast understands this. In other words, if you are fixated on something, it is easy to get side swiped if you fail to expand your vision in order to take in what's around you. Think about it.

Aside from learning how to expand your visual field, determining your dominant eye is another important element of visual training. Your dominant eye transmits and processes visual input a few milliseconds prior to the opposite eye. Make a steeple with your right and left index fingers, and tuck your thumb and other fingers into a fist. Extend your arms at shoulder height and frame a small object in the distance with your triangle. Close one eye and focus at the object. Whichever eye centers the object in the window of the steeple is your dominant eye.

Different types of eye movements are used to track various types of athletic movement.

- **Saccadic** eye movement is used in rapid scanning.

- **Vestibular-ocular** movements integrate eye movement with head movement and assist with balance.

- **Vergence** eye movements focus on objects moving in the distance.

- **Smooth pursuit** eye movements follow objects moving in slow motion.

Saccadic eye movement decreases with age. This can cause increased blinking, which may in turn cause errors in visual tracking. A study conducted in 1980 showed that anxiety will cause increased blinking in athletes. Since blinking causes the eyes to be closed for about one-tenth of a second, serious errors of visual judgment can occur.

Static visual acuity refers to the ability to the ability to discern stationary detail in an object. Some of the factors influencing static visual acuity are color, light, contrast and motion. While greater illumination can improve acuity, too much glare can interfere with it. Dynamic visual acuity refers to the ability to discern detail in objects in motion. While it varies with each individual, studies have shown that dynamic visual acuity improves with training.

While many people think of vision in relationship to the static activity of reading, there are many exercises that promote a more dynamic, sport-specific integration of vision and motion.

According to Dr. Barry Seiller, M.D., Director of Vision Training for the U.S. ski team, "Visual skills affect the skier's reaction time, balance, eye/hand/body coordination—all those skills that can make the difference between a good and a great run." Seiller asserts that skiers need to "shift visual gaze rapidly and smoothly from near-to-far and distant-to-close and detect changes in the terrain and snow conditions, often under adverse weather conditions." If you have ever attempted to ski a bump run in either flat light or in a whiteout, you would have to agree with him.

Dr. Seiller suggests practicing the following exercises for thirty minutes, three times a week:

- **Pencil push-ups:** Hold a pencil at arm's length. Focus on the pencil's number and move the pencil toward you. When the number blurs, extend your arm and begin again.

- **Vision in Motion:** While riding in a car, walking or going for a walk, try to read road signs, license plates, etc., on your far right or left, without moving your head. Perform the exercise for five minutes, rest five minutes and repeat.

- **On the Couch:** Turn on the TV and tune to the preview channel that lists texts on the screen. Simultaneously open a newspaper. Alternate between reading the screen and the newspaper texts. Gradually increase your speed.

FOURTEEN

Flexibility Fact and Fiction

Resistance is not futile, we're gonna win this thing,
humankind is too good; we're not a bunch of under-achievers!
We're going to stand up, and we're gonna be human beings.
We're going to get fired up about the real things,
the things that matter! Creativity, and the
dynamic human spirit that refuses to submit.

—RICHARD LINKLATER IN *WALKING LIFE*

Back in college, I used to teach yoga. I was so flexible that you could bend me, shape me any way you wanted me. As long as my students loved me, it was all right. One day, I enrolled in a dance course. Much to my dismay, I discovered that my dance instructor was not really impressed with my capacity to become a human Gumby. I still recall her words: "In fitness and in life, you should never be more flexible than you are strong. In other words, you should not be able to bend over backwards for anyone or anything unless you are strong enough to pull yourself back up."

When you hear the same thing twice in one year, you should listen. In a college kinesiology class, my instructor used me as a role model to show why hyper-mobility without the benefit of strength can destroy the integrity of the joints. Because of their sound advice,

I've managed to spend thirty-one years in the fitness industry, running marathons, teaching high impact aerobics, etc., before having even one serious injury.

Both my dance instructor and kinesiology professor were way ahead of their time. A good deal of research has indicated that being hyper-flexible is just as dangerous as being inflexible. Once a muscle has reached its absolute maximum length, any attempt to stretch the muscle further will only stretch the ligaments. This puts undue stress on the tendons. Here is something to think about: A ligament will tear if it is stretched more than six percent of its normal length. Even if your ligaments and tendons do not tear, overly loose joints will significantly increase your chance of injury.

The renowned sports coach Vern Gambetta has an interesting article on his Web site, entitled "Too Much, Too Loose." He cautions us with these words of wisdom: "Much of this controversy has arisen because the cult of flexibility that would lead us to believe that our athletes must become contortionists in order to prevent injuries and perform athletic movements."

Flexibility is defined as the range of motion available at each joint. But Gambetta believes that we must transcend this definition when we speak about flexibility as applied to sport performance. He redefines flexibility as being the largest dynamic range of motion that can be controlled.

"Mostability" is a term coined by the physical therapist and sports medicine expert Gary Gray. He defines mostability as "the ability to functionally take advantage of just the right amount of motion at just the right joint in just the right plane in just the right direction at just the right time."

Consider this: After any type of static stretch, your body is incapable of performing with top agility or maximal speed. This is because your muscles become less responsive to stimulation. When your muscles are less responsive to stimulation, there is less feedback to the nervous system. As a result, your coordination is compromised. Static stretches also reduce the force production of your muscles, which essentially makes them weaker. These statements have been backed by a considerable amount of research. Here are the highlights of some of the studies:

- **Three fifteen-second stretches** of the hamstrings, quadriceps, and calf muscles reduced the peak vertical velocity of a vertical jump in the majority of subjects.[1]

- **Maximal force** in knee flexion declined on the average by 7.3% and in knee extension by 8.1% after static stretching even though 10–15 minutes passed between stretching and the strength test.[2]

Today, I notice a paradox that occurs with flexibility training. Those who need it the least practice it with a frightening religious fervor, while those who need it the most avoid it like the plague. Indeed, flexibility is an important component of fitness, but how much flexibility do we really need? Furthermore, what kind of flexibility do we need?

When most people talk about flexibility, they are referring to what is known as "static" or "passive" flexibility. *Static flexibility* involves holding a stretch in a passive position for an extended period of time. This type of flexibility is highly beneficial for anyone who experiences excessive muscular tension. Many people, though, use static stretching as a means of practicing contortions. When you choose a flexibility exercise, ask yourself this question: How often will I need to use my body in this position? When you go skiing, do you sit on top of the slopes with your legs wrapped around you like a pretzel? I think not. I certainly hope not!

All of us can benefit from being both physically and mentally flexible. We can, however, either use this flexibility to enhance our agility as we become pliable in our movements through the situations that life presents to us, or we can choose to be static and passive

1. Knudson, D., K. Bennet, R. Corn, D. Leick, and C. Smith. 2000. "Acute Effects of Stretching Are Not Evident in the Kinematics of the Vertical Jump," *Research Quarterly for Exercise and Sport,* vol. 71, no. 1 [Supplement], p. A-30.

2. *Ibid.*

in our flexibility, yielding to whatever presents itself without taking action. Snow sports are action sports. They require us to be dynamic. Therefore, we need *dynamic flexibility.*

Dynamic flexibility is flexibility in motion. People with dynamic flexibility are able to connect their movements with fluidity and grace. Many people who have static flexibility lack this ability. Although this may seem paradoxical, there is a logical explanation. When you over-stretch your muscles in a non-functional manner, you sacrifice joint integrity. As a result, your body is unstable, and your transitional balance is compromised.

For snow sports, "transitional" is the operative word. You might be able to stand on one leg for an hour, but what happens when you need to dance? There is an intricate relationship between transitional balance, transitional strength and transitional flexibility. When someone has good transitional balance, his or her movements are in constant support by their deep core musculature. This is distinctly different from the tense, bracing action that people use when they are trying to hold themselves in one position without moving.

Transitional flexibility takes advantage of the joint mobility that is combined with the joint integrity achieved by strength training. The result is beautiful skiing. Techniques such as t'ai chi, Pilates and Feldenkrais Awareness Through Movement are effective ways to enhance dynamic flexibility. Ashtanga Yoga, a dynamic yoga system that incorporates strength, is also an effective way to enhance dynamic flexibility.

THE RESEARCH

Back in the Dark Ages, static stretching was considered a warm-up. Fortunately, we now know better. Although the jury is still out, there have been no studies that can conclusively prove that static stretch prior to sport will prevent injuries. In a study of 1538 Australian male army recruits, published in the February 2000 edition of *Medicine and Science in Sports and Exercise,* researchers randomly selected recruits and put them into two pre-exercise groups:

The stretch group performed stretching exercises following a warm-up.

The no-stretch or control group performed the same warm-up without the stretching exercises.

At the end of the twelve-week training program, the researchers found no significant difference in the number of injuries recorded in each of the two groups. This lead to the conclusion that "a typical muscle stretching protocol performed during pre-exercise warm-ups does not produce clinically meaningful reductions in risk of exercise related injury in army recruits."[3]

In another review, published in the August 2000 issue of *Physician and Sports Medicine*, authors Dr Ian Shrier and Kav Grossal found that stretching as part of a warm-up did not reduce the susceptibility to injury. These researchers found that "only warm-up is likely to prevent injury," and commented that if injury prevention is a primary objective of a warm-up routine, then athletes should "drop the stretching before exercise and increase warm-up."[4]

A snow-sport-specific warm-up allows you to gradually prepare the muscles, joints, lungs, heart and nervous system for a day on the slopes. A good warm-up will improve speed and coordination while preventing injuries. Your warm-up initiates communication with your nervous system. This enhanced communication improves sensory feedback from the muscles, tendons and joints, which in turn leads to better balance. A warm-up to a snow-sport enthusiast is like oil can to the Tin Woodsman. By lubricating the joints, you enhance muscular functionality.

On a cold morning on the slopes, a well-designed sport-specific warm-up will increase body heat. Sports medicine researchers have

3. Pope, R.P., Herbert, R.O. Kirwan, J.O., and Graham, B. J. (2000) "A Randomized trail of pre exercise stretching for prevention of lower limb injury" *Medicine and Science in Sports and Exercise* 32(2), p. 27–277.

4. Shrier, I. and Grossal, K. (2000) "Myths and Truths of Stretching" *The Physician and Sports Medicine* 28(8), p. 57–63.

indicated that optimal athletic performance is associated with higher muscle temperatures. The bodily functions needed for sports performance are dependent on temperature. As you start your dynamic warm-up, your temperature rises. This stimulates the lubrication of your joints by immersing them *synovial fluid*. Synovial fluid reduces joint and bone friction, thus allowing them to move with grace and fluidity.

FIFTEEN

Getting High
(Strategies for Snow Sports at Altitude)

Mountains have a way of dealing with overconfidence.

—HERMANN BUHL

I WANT TO TAKE YOU HIGHER

So you've heard the beck and call of the mountains, and you want to go big. The lure of skiing in Colorado, Utah, or certain parts of Europe holds the promise of unique excitement for sea-level city dwellers. The feeling of being on higher ground, almost up close and personal with the heavens, provides an exhilarating sensation that is second to none. Lest you be hasty in your travel plans, you should consider the hazards of high altitude. A trip to high country need not be dangerous, if rigorous precautions are taken.

HOW HIGH IS HIGH?

The following scale describes the various levels of altitude:

- **High:** 8,000–12,000 feet

- **Very High:** 12,000–18,000 feet

- **Extremely High:** Above 18,000 feet

As of yet, no study has been conclusive as to what factors influence a person's susceptibility to altitude sickness. Men and women of all ages and levels of fitness may or may not be susceptible. To further complicate matters, you may take one trip and have no symptoms, then return at a different time and get considerably ill.

While most people can travel to 8,000 feet without problem, if you rarely travel above sea level, it's best to be prudent in your preparations.

One of the great things about learning a snow sport is that it can inspire you to take winter vacations that will keep you in good shape! Our ski travels have brought us to destinations throughout the United States, Eastern and Western Canada, and Europe. The great thing about European ski travel is that in many cases, it is considered off-season for the airlines, so your tickets may be less expensive. One of the most fascinating trips we took was to Bormio, Italy. The town of Bormio is a medieval village that features a wonderful, historic hot spring. Bormio gives you the chance to have both an athletic and an educational vacation. For a small fee, you can take a day trip to the elegant St. Moritz, which would be a rather expensive destination if you were actually staying there. Bormio, on the other hand, is inexpensive. Since St. Moritz is at a higher altitude, spending time at Bormio would give you time to acclimate.

ALL I NEED IS THE AIR THAT I BREATHE

At sea level, oxygen concentration is at approximately 21% and barometric pressure is at 760mmHG. With the increase in altitude, oxygen concentration is unchanged, but the number of oxygen molecules per breath is significantly reduced. This is due to the fact that at 12,000 feet, barometric pressure is only 483mmHG, thereby giving even the most enthusiastic skier or hiker forty percent fewer oxygen molecules per breath.

To oxygenate the body properly, your breathing rate must increase. The added ventilation increase oxygen content in the blood, but not to the same concentration it was at sea level.

Unfortunately, whatever activity you are participating in will still require the same amount of oxygen, but your body must adjust to having less of it. High altitude can also cause fluid to leak from the capillaries, which in turn can cause fluid build up in the brain and lungs.

SO WHAT'S THE PROBLEM?

Persistent increased breathing results in the reduction of carbon dioxide in the blood. Since carbon dioxide build-up is the key signal to the brain that it is time to breathe. If levels are low, the drive to breathe is inhibited.

If you're awake, it isn't much trouble to breathe consciously. At night, however, an odd breathing pattern develops due to an alternating balancing act between two respiratory triggers. This periodic breathing consists of cycles of normal breathing, which gradually slows, followed by ten to fifteen seconds of breath holding, and a brief recovery period of accelerated breathing.

This isn't considered altitude sickness. While it usually improves with acclimatization, however, it rarely resolves till descent from altitude. Periodic breathing can be the cause of anxiety in a person who wakes up during the breath-holding phase, or in someone who awakens during the accelerated-breathing phase, believing that they are suffering from an extreme form of high altitude sickness.

GOTTA GO AGAIN!

Many changes occur in the body's fluid-balancing systems during acclimatization. As blood concentration is reset, a factor known as *altitude diuresis* causes the kidneys to excrete more fluid. As a result, frequent urination is normal. If this isn't happening, you are either dehydrated, or else you are not acclimating well. I've seen many sea-level students at Colorado's Copper Mountain refuse to drink water, for fear of "having to go" in the middle of class. Rest assured that your instructor would rather have you stop at one of the mountain's many rest rooms than have you carried down the hill in the ski patroller's sled due to high altitude sickness.

DEFINING ALTITUDE ILLNESS

In 1991, an International Hypoxia Symposium was held at Lake Louise in Alberta, Canada. A number of diagnostic definitions were adopted at the symposium.

Acute mountain sickness (AMS) is characterized by:

- Appetite loss, nausea or vomiting
- Fatigue and/or weakness
- Light headedness
- Dizziness
- Insomnia
- Confusion
- Altered Gait

There are a number of ways to avoid AMS:

- Spend a day at a lower altitude before proceeding to your higher destination.
- Sleep at a lower altitude
- Avoid alcohol and caffeine
- Stay hydrated
- Avoid sleeping pills
- Avoid narcotic pain medications
- Use caution when gaining altitude

If you are experiencing any of the symptoms of AMS, descent is crucial. Failure to do so can result in a more serious case of acute mountain sickness.

- **High-Altitude Cerebral Edema** occurs when AMS is not treated. The fluid build-up causes the brain to swell. This causes extreme disorientation and a lack of coordination. At this point, delaying descent can be fatal.

- **High-Altitude Pulmonary Edema** is the most severe form of AMS. Its symptoms include:

  - Difficulty breathing at rest
  - Extreme fatigue
  - Cough, possibly with pinkish emissions
  - Gurgling
  - Chest tightness
  - Blue lips and/or finger-nails

MEDICAL TREATMENTS AND PREVENTIVE METHODS

Diamox

Diamox is the most commonly prescribed drug for the prevention of altitude sickness. While it is usually effective, it should be avoided by anyone who is allergic to sulfa drugs. Its side effects include tingling of the fingers. Some people complain that Diamox makes carbonated drinks and beer taste weird.

Ginkgo Biloba: Lest You Forget

In 2000, research performed at Pike's Peak concluded that 120 mg of ginkgo biloba taken five days prior to ascent reduced both the incidence and severity of AMS. Since ginkgo is also known to improve memory, at the very least, taking ginkgo may make your trip a memorable experience.

Viagra: Getting Up and High

Perhaps the most unusual preventive method that is currently being researched is Viagra. The low oxygen levels found at high altitude can cause a narrowing of the pulmonary arteries. Viagra, which improves erectile dysfunction by widening the arteries in the penis, also widens the pulmonary arteries.

Dr. Jean-Paul Richalet and his colleagues wanted to see if Viagra helped prevent high-altitude health conditions. Twelve men, averaging age twenty-nine, volunteered for the experiment. None of them were used to high altitudes.

The study began at sea level, where baseline measurements were taken. Then participants spent a day at a higher altitude in Chamonix. The next day, they were taken 10,000 feet higher by helicopter to Observatoire Vallot, located just below the summit of Mont Blanc. This is the highest point in Western Europe. They remained in the mountain observatory for five days. While riding stationary bikes, they filled out surveys that checked for AMS. Half the group received Viagra; the other, a placebo.

After two days, the Viagra group's blood pressure began to normalize, while the placebo groups stayed high. Keep in mind that these studies are in their preliminary stages. More research is needed before people start popping Viagra prior to their spring break Colorado ski trips. Considering that the ratio of males to females in Colorado is about five to one, this could be an especially bad idea.

Head to the Bars

While oxygen bars are the current trend in high-altitude ski areas, they are not without controversy. The Food and Drug Administration has determined that any type of oxygen administered by another person is considered a drug and should only be prescribed and administered by a medical professional. Keep in mind that high-altitude ski areas have emergency clinics that will deliver legitimate forms of oxygen right to your doorstep, should you find yourself plagued by High-Altitude Cerebral Edema.

High/Low, High/Low, Elevation's Good to Know

While it's nice to know that these services exist, prevention is always preferable. Even in high country, some ski areas are at a lower altitude than others. In Colorado, Vail is at the lowest. You can also opt to stay in Denver, and take the ski train to Winter Park. That way, you'll be sleeping at a lower altitude. In Utah, the Park City area resorts are at the lowest elevation. Just a bit of research, along with taking some precautions, will help you stay healthy in high country.

SIXTEEN

ACL Injury
(When Bad Injuries Happen to Good Athletes)

> Suffering produces endurance,
> and endurance produces character,
> and character produces hope.
>
> —St. Paul (Romans 5:3-4)

Here comes a subject that is near and dear to my heart. Many skiers live in fear of the dreaded ACL injury. Others will say things like, "Don't worry; there are great surgical techniques that will fix any ACL tear."

Be that as it may, ACL surgery is no picnic. A good ski-fitness plan, excellent technique, and well-functioning equipment may prevent ACL injury. In this chapter, I'm presenting you with a well-designed injury prevention plan. This plan, though, should be accompanied by a reasonable, non-competitive attitude. Be sure to read the next chapter so that you can learn from my mistakes.

By now you may be wondering what this "ACL" thing is. The anterior cruciate ligament (ACL) connects the femur to the tibia at the center of the knee. It is responsible for limiting rotation and forward motion of the tibia. An estimated 80,000–100,000 ACL tears occur annually in the general population.

For the most part, torn ACLs are considered non-contact injuries. They usually occur during:

- Planting and Cutting Moves
- Straight Leg Landing from Jumps
- Pivoting with Hyperextension

Upon injuring your ACL, you will usually hear a loud popping noise. Seeking immediate medical care is crucial.

ACL deficient knees or reconstructed ACLs have a one hundred and five times greater chance of developing osteoarthritis. Even with the best health insurance plan, the surgery is costly. While the post-operative prognosis is usually positive, you are probably looking at a six-month recovery period, with the first month being characterized by a good deal of physical pain and depression. Given the financial, physical and emotional stress that ACL injury can put on a skier, prevention is crucial. How rigorous should your prevention plan be? That depends upon your susceptibility.

ARE YOU SUSCEPTIBLE?

Some people can participate in a sport for years, and never damage their ACL. Others have had three or four ACL reconstructions. What determines susceptibility?

You are female. This is not a sexist statement. Statistics don't lie. If you are female, you are probably asking "why me?" The following factors contribute to a woman's susceptibility to ACL injury:

- **"Q" angle:** The Q angle refers to the quadriceps angle, or the angle between the hip and the knee. Since it is steeper in women, they are more prone to having the kneecap slide, thereby causing injury.

- **Less androgen:** Having less androgen means that women are often less prone to developing large muscles. Muscle fiber helps protect the joints and connective tissue. Female athletes are subject to the same torque forces in their knee as men. If the muscle is not strong enough to protect the joint, the kneecap will be even more prone to sliding.

Jump landing tactics: Women do not bend their knees as much as men when landing from a jump. This increases knee joint pressure.

- **Pivoting tactics:** Women turn and pivot in a more erect position. Bending at the knee and hip reduces ACL stress.

- **Quadricep/hamstring imbalance:** Women use their quads more then their hamstrings when landing and changing direction. As the quadriceps contract, the hamstrings will stretch and relax. A stretched muscle produces less force. If the knee is not sufficiently flexed, there will be increased force on the shinbone. This can cause an ACL tear. It's extremely important to realize that anyone, male or female, whose quadricep muscles are significantly stronger than their hamstrings, may be highly susceptible to ACL injury.

- **Narrow intercondylar notch:** This is a controversial theory, but worth examining. The intercondylar notch is at the end of the thigh. This is where the anterior and posterior cruciate ligaments form an x. It has been speculated that since women have a narrow notch, it predisposes them to ACL injury.

- **Estrogen and joint laxity:** Female hormones often give women natural joint and muscular flexibility. Unfortunately, this often leads to hyper mobility. The current trend toward extreme yoga practices that encourage contortion, as opposed to functional, dynamic flexibility may be one of the key reasons that women are suffering more ACL injuries. Keep in mind, there has been no study that has successfully concluded that pre-sport stretching prevents injury, but many studies have demonstrated that excessive pre-activity stretching can actually cause injury. In 1988, a Swedish study of 108 female soccer players demonstrated that the players were more susceptible to injury during the pre-menstrual and menstrual stages of their cycles. It's interesting to note that injuries were reduced when oral contraceptives were administered.

- **Foot factors:** A common phrase used in sports medicine is, "Don't look just at the site of the crash." In the case of an ACL tear, the muscles around the knee are not the only ones to be considered. You also need to take a look at the feet. The three most common foot factors related to ACL injury are:

  1. **Pronation** (rotation of the medial bones of the midtarsal region of the foot inward and downward so that in walking the foot tends to come down on its inner margin)

  2. **Limited dorsi flexion** (ability to curl toes toward shin)

  3. **Flat feet.** Landing flat-footed from a jump can cause ACL injury. The proper landing progression is:

     a. Toe

     b. Ball

     c. Heel

     d. Squat

- **Lack of neuromuscular coordination:** Even recreational athletes with minimal muscular imbalances may be susceptible to ACL tears due to faulty muscular firing patterns. The hamstrings may be strong, but if they don't fire at the exact right moment, they will not protect the ACL. Training the chain, referring to the kinetic chain, which describes the sequence of muscular contractions in any movement pattern and which we talked about earlier, helps prevent this. Cutting edge sport fitness professionals seek out training patterns that mimic the kinetic chain sequences of specific sports.

- **Insufficient balance and stability:** Prior to any foot strike, your deep core muscles must to stabilize the sacroiliac (SI) joint. If this does not happen, the SI joint is destabilized, causing a misalignment of the femurs connection to the pelvis, which in turn misaligns the knee.

- **Lack of proprioception:** Proprioception refers to the awareness of your body's position in space. Poor proprioception will make you unaware of the terrain below your feet. This lack of awareness can cause you to misjudge your movement patterns, thereby setting you up for injury.

- **Tight hip flexors:** Tight hip flexors are usually accompanied by a weak gluteus. If your gluteus is weak, your quadriceps need to work harder, which in turn causes a hamstring/quadriceps imbalance, which sets you up for injury.

- **Tight illiotibial band:** The IT band runs down the side of your leg. If it's tight, it inhibits the workings of the *vatsus medialis,* the muscle above the knee responsible for correct knee tracking. Incorrect knee tracking can cause injury.

- **Weak eccentric strength:** Since ACL injuries happen in the eccentric or lengthening phase of muscular contraction, lack of eccentric strength can cause injury.

Poor technique and malfunctioning equipment: Even if none of the above factors are present, poor technique and malfunctioning equipment can lead to ACL injury. The Vermont Ski Safety Association has outlined the key technical faults that set a skier up for injury:

- Attempting to get up while still moving after a fall.

- Attempting a recovery from an off-balance position.

- Attempting to sit down after losing control.

- Uphill arm back.

- Skier off-balance to the rear.

- Hips below the knees.

- Uphill ski unweighted.

- Weight on the inside edge of downhill ski tail. Upper body is generally facing the downhill ski.

PREVENTION PLAN

If you are a serious recreational athlete, your first step is to find a certified fitness professional specializing in sports conditioning and postural alignment analysis. Pilates instructors and instructors certified by The National Academy of Sports Medicine are usually your best bet. These professionals will create programs based on your specific misalignments and muscular imbalances. Make sure that your trainer pays particular attention to your pelvic, knee and foot alignment, since these areas have the greatest influence on the ACL.

Should you choose to create your own program, there are a number of things to consider.

- **Train barefoot, at least sometimes:** It's no surprise that dancers and martial artists, who train barefoot, have the lowest incidence of ACL tears. Skiers, whose boots restrict proprioception, have the highest. Since martial arts forms such as judo teach their participants how to fall, such classes can be effective for cross training.

- **Integrate strength training with balance:** Devices such as the stability ball, wobble board, Dyna-Disc, Bosu and so on are used by the top athletic teams. You should use them, too.

- **Work your hamstrings:** review the stability ball hamstring curl in chapter twenty. This is one of the best hamstring exercises for snow sliders.

- **Avoid the leg extension machine:** This machine can apply shearing forces to the knee, making it more susceptible to ACL injury.

- **Practice closed-chain exercise:** Closed-chain exercises keep your foot in a closed position, i.e., in contact with the floor. This incorporates the use of more muscle groups, while lessening the shearing forces on the knee present in open chain exercises such as the leg extension. Examples of closed chain exercises are the squat and the leg press.

- **Practice plyometrics:** Plyometrics teach participants proper jump-landing mechanisms. Since this involves landing with knees flexed, plyometrics are an excellent way to achieve sufficient hamstring strength.

While many people refer to sport conditioning as "off-season training," this is a big mistake. Conditioning should be a year-round event. Unfortunately, even the best conditioning program will not protect you from ACL injury if your athletic technique is insufficient, and/or your equipment is not working properly. You can be an excellent skier, but if you are practicing your sport at the end of the day (when most sport injuries occur), you may still be injured. Checking your equipment is also crucial. A binding that fails to release can turn a benign fall into a serious injury.

In the event that you *do* tear your ACL, most people opt for surgery. If this happens, your surgeon will tell you to start physical therapy within two days post-op. Heed this advice. Failure to do so will result in a loss of range of motion.

Always get your physician's approval prior to starting any new exercise program.

Play safe!

SEVENTEEN

Healing the Body, Healing the Soul

Fear...the right and necessary counterweights to that courage
which urges men skyward, and protects them from self-destruction.

—HEINRICH HARRER

The information I presented to you in the previous chapter was the type of stuff I had been writing about for years. Having spent most of my fitness career with an uncanny resistance to injury, I never believed that I would one day become the victim of the very injury I was writing about.

Many skiers have a cavalier attitude about ACL injuries. At the risk of presenting myself as a drama queen, I'll tell you that tearing my ACL was one of the worst things that have ever happened in my life. After the injury, I felt like I was a fraud. What business did I have telling people how to prevent injuries or stay in shape? Picabo Street, the ski racer, has a habit of saying "When you're hurt, you're dirt." Perhaps that's a bit extreme. I will tell you this, though. My body healed from the ACL surgery a lot faster than my mind and soul. The emotional impact of being hurt while doing something I loved was as strong as having my heart broken by a lover. Yet looking back, I now realize that the injury was inevitable. Had I heeded the warning signs, it could have been prevented. Here is the story.

During my first year in Colorado, October brought early snowfall.

My ski season had begun. Every Wednesday, I would ski at Loveland with some of the top pros in Summit County. While I was gaining confidence, unfortunately, I was beginning to lose my common sense. One of my rare wipeouts caused a minor medial lateral ligament (MCL) strain. I recall the words of the x-ray technician: "You won't get bragging rights for this injury." There is more seriousness than silliness to this statement. Amongst recreational skiers, injury has received a sick sort of status. In the past, I'd been told that since I'd never been injured, I wasn't a "real skier."

Since my fitness level kept the MCL injury from being as severe as it could have been, I neglected to see it as a warning sign that I was pushing too hard too soon. Nonetheless, it healed quickly. I've always been cautious about maintaining a balance between strength and flexibility. Consequently, I don't have the same hyper mobility issues prevalent in women whose only fitness regimen involves flexibility exercise. My doctor thought that I was knowledgeable enough to do my own rehab, but he advised me to avoid yoga stretches until the injury was completely healed. He responded positively when I told him that I didn't practice yoga. My joints showed a tendency toward hyper-flexibility. If I had been practicing any extreme adductor stretches, my MCL would have been torn, rather than strained. Having strengthened my adductors on the slide board, the abductor/adductor machine, and isometrically with the Pilates fitness circle, I protected myself from a more serious injury.

Three weeks after my injury, I was skiing again.

When Copper Mountain opened, I began taking lessons with my friend Michael on a weekly basis.

Although I was skiing terrain that I never imagined possible, to say that I was on a continuous lift ride toward improvement would be untrue. There were good days. There were bad days. The bad days left me angry with myself. Mike tried to convince me that my belief that my progress should be linear was unrealistic. As a fitness instructor, I should have understood the concept of physical and mental plateaus.

Still, I couldn't help but feel that since he was putting so much energy into teaching me, the least I could do was ski correctly, darn it! On my bad days, I felt as if I was an instructor's worst nightmare. As a movement professional, I hated this feeling. In retrospect, I now realize that my obsession with rapid improvement led me to make some foolish choices. I began to train harder rather than smarter.

Each day after I finished teaching, I contemplated doing my own workout. My hands-on teaching style didn't supply me with a workout that could sufficiently challenge my high level of fitness. I knew darned well that skiing was not giving me the sort of aerobic workout I was used to, but the icy conditions on the streets of Summit County made me afraid to go running. In the past, I'd been afraid to ski because I didn't want to incur an injury that would keep me from running. Now I didn't want to run, for fear that I would fall on the ice, and injure myself for skiing. This was my first big mistake.

In the past, my aerobic conditioning had helped me stay alert for an entire ski day, sometimes till after the lifts were closed. That season, however, I began to lose mental energy at around two-thirty in the afternoon. I also realized that I should have been doing some additional strength training. Given the choice between the gym and the mountain, however, the mountain won every time.

Here is one of the cardinal rules of conditioning: Your workouts must be progressive. My teaching helped me maintain a basic level of fitness, but it was not rigorous enough to support the demands I was putting on my body.

Let me tell you about these demands. I began skiing five to seven days a week. While I knew that I should have been practicing my skills on easier terrain, I stopped skiing green runs altogether. This caused a subtle set back in my technique. Since I was always skiing "on the edge," I was beginning to redevelop the defensiveness that I had worked so hard to get rid of. Unfortunately, I had become addicted to the adrenaline rush of advanced skiing. Having once been an overly cautious skier, I was now throwing caution to the wind.

The first time I skied down a bump run I felt as if I had been crowned Queen of the Slopes. I had skied bumps before, but they were far less challenging than the bumps at Copper. Although these bumps were somewhat scary, I was amazed at how well my instructor's teaching had prepared me for them. My aspirations to become a bumpin' babe lead me to an uncharacteristic sense of confidence. I went from being a mogul phobic to a mogul maniac.

That winter, a flu that we called "the Summit County crud" ran rampant throughout the area. Even with my unusually high immunity, I caught it in January and was on the verge of catching it again in March. From my days as a marathon runner, I knew that frequent colds and flu were the signs of overtraining, but once again, I ignored the warnings that my body was sending me.

On the morning of March 6th, I woke up feeling a bit queasy. It was Sunday, however, and I wanted to go to class. We warmed up on a blue run, and regrouped at the bottom of the trail. Suddenly, an instructor skied down with this incredible skier. She was easily a level eight or nine, so I was surprised that the instructor told her she would be right for our level-six class. All of us cringed. We now had someone we had to keep up with.

For most of the day, she skied at twice our speed. Some of us became frustrated while trying to keep up with her, and began displaying our old bad habits. At about two-thirty, we skied down a black-diamond run called Hallelujah. I was thrilled that, even in my less than confident state of mind, I was able to ski it in relatively good form. Little did I know that it would soon become, as Leonard Cohen says, "a cold and broken Hallelujah." Mike asked us what we'd like to ski for our last run.

Our hotshot skier replied, "Let's do another bump run."

Mike looked skeptical. He said, "Any one of you can veto this idea."

None of us spoke up. I really wanted to ski a groomer, but I was afraid of being the class wimp. Besides, we were going to ski a blue bump run. No problem. We proceeded down Upper Main Vain.

Our advanced skier went down at mach ten. Two other classmates followed swiftly. Only two of us were left. Unfortunately, the other woman in our class had an annoying habit of hitting people on

A "groomer" is slang for a slope that has been combed over by grooming equipment, resulting in a smooth, wavy surface that some people call corduroy. A groomed surface is the easiest surface to ski or ride on.

bump runs. I always let her ski ahead of me. Although she usually complained to Mike about his class not being challenging enough, she too was having problems on this run.

Nonetheless, I felt guilty about holding everyone up. It looked as if she was about to finally start her run, so I thought I was good to go. Unfortunately, I broke one of the cardinal rules of skiing: I focused on *her,* as opposed to where I wanted to go.

As I got closer, I realized that she had chosen to stand still like a deer caught in the headlights. I was close to the edge of the trail, so my choices were limited. Given that I was tired, instead of turning my skis up the hill to avoid her, I leaned into the hill.

Down I went.

My fall involved a twisting action. I was sporting a pair of heavy Volants whose bindings failed to release. This was just another example of my hubris. Having reached the "golden age," I should have had my din settings adjusted so my ski boots would release properly, but I was feeling too young to follow the rules. Unfortunately, as I tried to stand up, my left leg buckled underneath me.

Mike called the ski patrol. It was time for Lisa's first sled ride. Arriving at the Copper clinic, I received the bad news. It was probable that I'd torn my ACL and done damage to my medial meniscus and MCL. Later, an MRI would confirm this diagnosis. My surgery was scheduled for March 16th.

I began to do pre-operation exercises to increase my range of motion. Different surgeons have different opinions on when surgery should be performed. Many believe that you should pre-habilitate and only have surgery once your range of motion is recovered. In Summit County, they want you in there as soon as possible.

My doctor decided on an allograft. The patellar graft can make kneeling difficult and the hamstring graft can cause an imbalance between hamstrings and quads.

NEVER A GOOD TIME

Must find ways to keep laughing, must smile, must not cry.

While there's never a good time to get injured, this couldn't have happened at a worse time. My husband Mark was scheduled to return to Boston to prepare our condo for resale. He was able to delay it for a week, but time was running short. I couldn't teach, but we had to pay rent and utilities on the studio. We had already incurred considerable debt from starting up a new business. Insurance deductibles had to be met. Mark had a part-time IT job and was teaching two days a week at Breckenridge. To complicate matters, Mark tore his MCL while teaching a class. Put simply, we were broke. The condo needed to be sold ASAP.

Mike volunteered to walk our greyhound, Giselle, feed our cats, and take me to surgery. At six-thirty that morning he drove me to Vail Valley Medical Center. A few hours post-op, I awakened in the recovery room. The nurse asked me to rate my pain on a scale of one to ten. It was a definite six. They gave me some pain medication. I noticed that there was an oxygen tube up my nose. What fresh hell is this? I wondered. (Mother Mary had not yet arrived in my time of trouble to give me solace, so in my hour of darkness, I had to rely on Dorothy Parker.)

It seemed that I had an atelectasis, a partial collapse of a lung, sometimes brought on by general anesthesia. I had to practice coughing, and breathing into some weird tubular device. A screen above my bed indicated what my oxygen level was. It had to be at ninety before I was allowed to go home. Mike observed the screen with anxiety, as if watching a falling stock market. My oxygen level stayed stubbornly in the seventies. Finally, at five-fifteen that evening, I was sent home with an oxygen tank.

When we got into the car, I began to talk, but apparently the pain meds were causing me to speak in *non sequiturs*. Since I don't take drugs, and I rarely drink, the medication had a powerful effect on me. I find it hard to believe that some people voluntarily induce this state of mind.

A LONG DARK NIGHT OF THE SOUL

The trauma began when I had to walk upstairs, using my crutches. Unfortunately, my sense of light-headedness made me terrified of using them. Mike reminded me that the physical therapist had said it was okay to go up and down on my butt. I took this suggestion enthusiastically. As he observed my new way of getting upstairs, he remarked, "Hey, you've developed a new triceps exercise."

Always the optimist.

A word to the wise: Do not spend the night of your surgery by yourself. Friends had offered to stay with me, but I was too proud to accept. My low oxygen level, combined with the effect of the medication, created a frightening anxiety. For the first time in years, my balance and proprioception were way off. The situation was exacerbated by the fact that my appetite was nonexistent. As a result, I barely had enough strength to get out of bed. Each trip to the bathroom was an odyssey of terror.

While my level of fitness has given me an unusually high pain threshold, in the week that followed my surgery, pain would take on a whole new meaning. Faced with this new feeling of fragility, any sort of movement frightened me. The couch became a cocoon of comfort. The Lifetime Movie Network became my best friend.

Looking back, the psychological changes I went through during this time were disturbing. I began to lose my ability to communicate either verbally or in writing. While I am known for my long emails and phone conversations with friends, I had no desire to connect with anyone, using any medium of communication. I was hardly eating, but since I wasn't exercising, I believed that I was getting ridiculously fat. When friends came to walk my greyhound Giselle, I hid under the covers so that they would not see how I looked.

Loss of appetite is not uncommon post-anesthesia. My distorted body image did not help this. I began to consciously eat less, which exacerbated my chronic fatigue and dizziness.

Although most orthopedic surgeons believe that physical therapy should begin two days post-op, I was in no condition to leave the house. I finally scheduled a visit one week later, on the same day as my doctor's appointment. Scheduling the appointment was easier than going to it. I hadn't left the house for a week, and I had developed a strange sense of agoraphobia. My terror of leaving home would continue for another few weeks.

The doctor's visit brought bad news. My oxygen level was still unusually low. I would have to remain on the tank. More bad news came from the PT. My range of motion was abysmal. Nobody at the hospital had warned me against putting a pillow under my knee. Doing so keeps your knee in flexion, making extension close to impossible. The pillow is supposed to go under your ankle. Unfortunately, this provides no pain relief whatsoever. The situation was made worse by the fact that I waited one week before going to PT. Also, my insurance did not cover a CPM, a continuous passive motion machine, often-used post-op. Friends who had used this machine regained their range of motion a whole lot faster.

In the weeks that followed, I would begin to develop a strong sense of empathy with my most unfit students. For the first time in my life, I dreaded being in a gym-like environment. Not only was I not in a position of control, I was the least fit person in the room. My first breakdown occurred when the therapist asked me to try to pedal the bike at a full range of motion. It was impossible. Later, when she tried to flex or extend my knee for me, my screams terrified the other patients. I was convinced that I would never heal.

While common and understandable, this attitude is dangerous. I needed to find ways to motivate myself to heal. The director of the local theatre company was holding auditions for *Midsummer Night's Dream*. I emailed him and asked if he thought I was ready for Shakespeare. He responded by telling me to prepare two monologues, whether I was ready or not. "You need to start being someone other than an injured person."

It's interesting to note that the mental process involved in preparing an audition piece for Titania, queen of the fairies, had a similar outcome to the theatrical exercises I had used on the slopes. A fairy does not move like a gimp. In the hours I spent working on the monologue, I felt no pain.

Eventually I became more confident about taking the healing process into my own hands. Although I was advised not to begin teaching, I knew that teaching would be the only thing that would motivate me to get better. Additionally, I began to develop my own rehab methods.

Snow-sport instructors often debate whether fitness prevents ACL injury. I can only respond from personal experience. I spent over thirty years in the fitness industry without ever being injured. When I was at my highest level of fitness, I was never injured, even though my skiing skills were abysmal. My injury occurred when my ski skills were at their highest, but my fitness level was at its lowest. Meanwhile, my students were having fewer injuries than they had ever experienced in a season. If there is anything positive that came from this experience, it was the knowledge that the Snow Condition program really does work, as long as you consistently practice it. Learn from my mistakes. When you finish this chapter, check out the Snow Condition program in Part Two.

With getting back into condition in mind, I began to work out with a vengeance.

THE ACL REHAB PLAN: HOW LISA GOT HER GROOVE BACK

Your first priority after ACL surgery is regaining range of motion. While static stretching is definitely required, in my case, dynamic flexibility was the most helpful. Every case is different, so please consult with your doctor or surgeon before beginning any exercise program. Many of my abdominal exercises involve:

- Lying on my back.

- Heels on the stability ball.

- Flexing or extending either one leg or both while performing crunches or upper body rotations.

- Prone exercises on the ball were also extremely helpful, particularly the knee pull in the stability ball exercise chapter. A quick review:

1. Lie prone with your belly on the ball and hands on the floor, feet off the floor.

2. Inhale to prepare.

3. Exhale as you bend your knees and try to bring them toward your chest.

4. Keep your abdominals drawn in.

5. Focus on the ball.

6. Inhale to straighten your legs.

This was extremely helpful for me at that time because I was able to see my progress as my knee began to regain its range of motion. Flexion in the prone position is one of the most challenging things to do post-ACL surgery. I found that the assisted stretches performed by my "physical terrorist" were more painful than I could tolerate. The foam roller quadricep stretches I describe in the chapter twenty-five were an extremely helpful Plan B:

• Lie prone with quadriceps on foam roller.

• Maintain core control by drawing abdominals in.

• Foam roller quadriceps stretch movement: roll from pelvic bone to knee.

• If a "tender point" is found, stop rolling, and rest on the tender point until pain decreases by seventy-five percent.

After the foam roller, I would lie on my back and flex and extend the leg against the resistance of a theraband. Then I would turn over and flex the knee with the help of a stretch cord.

As I began to heal, I decided to amp up my post-rehab routine. My intuition told me that I needed a program that used dynamic range of motion exercises as opposed to static stretching. At the recreation center, I would use the elliptical machine, followed by the recumbent bicycle.

I also included lateral walking on the treadmill, which provided dynamic strength for the adductors and abductors. This was important for preventing re-injury of the MCL and meniscus.

1. Set the machine on an incline.

2. Stand sideways with your left foot uphill and your right foot downhill.

3. Hold the rails until you are confident about your balance.

4. Start the machine at a slow pace.

5. Step up with your left foot.

6. Bring your right foot up to meet it.

7. Perform for five minutes.

8. Pause machine and switch sides.

One of the important things verified for me during the rehab process was the importance of working my body as a whole. Early traditional physical therapy involved the use of muscle isolation exercise. The healing process, though, was expedited once I began to allow my injured leg to "play along" with the rest of my body.

Before long I was in good shape. When three of Summit and Eagle Counties' top instructors, however, became injured in the early season, I took it as a sign to wait a bit before I made my "comeback."

EPILOGUE: THE COMEBACK KID

I returned to skiing eight months post-surgery. Perhaps the hardest part about getting back is the knowledge that the graft is not totally healed until one year post-op. I was tentative, to say the least, because I did not know what would be safe. My plan was to start on very flat terrain. The terrain I chose, though, was too flat to accurately assess my skill level, so I moved up to easy blue trails. All was well until early season conditions turned a trail I had frequently skied into a mogul field. Panic set in quickly. I was not ready to ski moguls. I chose to sideslip the entire run.

Fortunately, the next few days were better. In fact, I was amazed at how fast the improvements were happening. I was still somewhat tentative, though, since I didn't know how safe it was to get up on edge. As a result, I found myself using a bit too many rotary movements.

One week later, Weems Westfeldt contacted me. Weems has developed a learning system that he calls The Sports Diamond. He was confident that the principles of the system would be helpful for my "comeback," so he offered to come to Breckenridge to ski with me.

The sage of skiing had some sound advice. Weems believes that skiers who reach the advanced intermediate stage should broaden their learning focus. Unfortunately, this is when they sometimes choose to obsess on one aspect of skiing, such as bumps or steeps. This often leads to burnout or injury. The Diamond system encourages skiers to view the sport holistically. It is built on four foundations of sport competency:

1. Power embraces the technical and biomechanical aspects of sport performance.

2. Purpose defines your strategy and tactics on the hill.

3. Touch strengthens your spiritual connection with the sport.

4. Will encompasses your commitment to your chosen strategy.

These foundations had a strong influence on my re-education. His first step, however, was to adjust my attitude. Prior to riding the lift, I warned him that I had reverted to level-three skiing skills. After observing me, he commented that I was a level-six skier with a level-three mindset. My skis were parallel. The only reason that I was not getting high up on my edges was that I was skiing very slowly.

My skiing was what Weems described as "positional." My knees were in a perpetually flexed position. Weems gave me two movements that radically changed my skiing. He encouraged me to extend my legs between edge changes and add pressure to the big toe of the outside ski.

All of a sudden, I took off with complete confidence.

Later, I confided that this confidence frightened me. I felt that since I had been highly confident about my skills before I had been hurt, I would be better off if I remained tentative. This is apparently a common attitude among people who have been injured. Weems gave me something interesting to think about: *The past is not the future.*

With this in mind, we formed a game plan. I was to find the black part of every blue or green slope. Even when skiing out from the cafeteria, if there is an inch of a section that has the pitch of a double black diamond, I should ski that section. Look for small bumps on an easy run. Play with different speeds. Contrary to my belief, it was not necessary for me to stay on extremely easy terrain. I did not need to try to get back to where I was before, however.

That being said, the emotionally and financially expensive lessons learned from my injury have caused me to rethink my attitude about skiing. I loved the sport because of the sense of freedom it provided. I eventually became a slave, however, to my own competitive attitude and failed to see that I was on the fast road to burnout.

There are many people who will tell you that if you do not ski the most challenging terrain as quickly as possible, you are not improving, and are not really having fun. I truly believe that some people actually give up the sport because they buy into this attitude. Alpine skiing, however, provides an enjoyable experience for thrill seekers and cruisers alike. Choose your pleasure, but do not allow it to become an obsession.

Keep in mind that this may be easier said than done. Adrenaline can be addictive. During my years as a marathon runner, I had seen this happen to friends and students. My female running friends would run in Central Park during the late hours of the evening, even though it was common knowledge that it wasn't safe. Other friends would run when they were ill or injured. Unfortunately, I failed to see this happening to myself. Before I knew it, I had crossed the fine line between being adventurous and being downright reckless.

Looking back, I find it interesting to note that during this period of time I was treading on emotionally as well as physically dangerous terrain. The same sort of adrenaline addiction I had experienced on the slopes carried over into my life. As a result, although I had been in great shape for most of my life, the healing process after my surgery was slower than it should have been. My body simply refused to heal until I nursed the emotional wounds I had suffered throughout that year.

Just as we strive for physical balance and proprioception in our bodies, we need to keep track of our emotional ecology and balance. Balance in skiing is simply a reflection of who we are within.

In order to move beyond the emotional scars I had suffered as a result of the injury, there were two important things with which I needed to come to terms:

1. I was hurt while engaging in an activity about which I was passionate. This is almost as emotionally painful as being hurt by a lover. Our passions make us vulnerable. We can choose to live without passion, and that may keep us "safe"—unless, of course, we eventually die of boredom.

2. I was hurt while I was with someone who usually made me feel safe. One of the reasons I chose Mike as an instructor was that I always felt safe in his presence. We are, however, ultimately responsible for our own safety. I had neglected to care for my body in a way that I knew would prevent injury. Neither the presence of a trusted instructor nor a prayer to a higher being can make up for that total disregard for my own well-being. God, and ski instructors, help those who help themselves!

These days, the butterflies, which had taken a brief vacation, have returned to my stomach. They begin their dance at the start of every lift ride. Rather than chase them away, I simply encourage them to dance in formation.

PART TWO

Body
(The Snow Condition Workout)

Introduction

If you've reached this point in the book, hopefully I've inspired you to take up a snow sport and engage in a fitness program that will enhance your snow-sliding skills. The exercises in this section correspond to the exercise modules in the previous chapters. While it may be tempting to jump ahead to the "fun stuff" on the Bosu, balance boards, Dyna-discs, etc., it is important to begin with a solid foundation. If you master the core-essential, snowprioception, postural and foot-and-ankle exercises prior to "playing with the toys," you'll be working in better form once you attempt the more challenging exercises.

While it is impossible to create an exact replica of a snow-sliding experience on dry land, you can practice skiing or riding in the theater of your mind. As you practice the exercises, imagine the snow falling around you, and how the wind feels as it passes above your head. You can intensify the experience by watching a skiing or snowboarding video as you exercise.

Above all, remember that since snow sports are fun, your sport fitness program should also be fun. Much to my editor's dismay, I've provided you with an overwhelming variety of exercises. The best exercises are the ones that you enjoy the most.

Here are some key pointers to remember when performing the exercises:

- Use the breathing techniques. In most cases, I will have you inhale in preparation and then exhale as you perform the movement. As you exhale, imagine that you are blowing the air out of a balloon and hollowing your belly.

- Engage your core muscles throughout all the exercises. Your belly button is the ignition button. Pressing it in gives energy and support to all of your movements. Keep in mind that this is very different from yoga exercise, where at times you will allow the belly to become extremely loose and flaccid. When practicing balance training exercise, you need your core muscles engaged in *both* phases of the movement. Once you develop an awareness of your deep core muscles, try this: On the first phase of the movement, concentrate on drawing your navel toward your spine. Then on the return phase of the exercise, think about those Kegels. Imagine that you are drawing your pelvic floor upward like a hammock.

- Only perform as many movements as you can perform in good form.

- Always check with your doctor before beginning an exercise program.

EIGHTEEN

Core–Essential and Snowprioception Exercises

POSTURE EXERCISES

CORE-ESSENTIAL AND SNOWPRIOCEPTION EXERCISES

The Four-Point Drawing-in Maneuver

1. Kneel on all fours.

2. Hips are lined up with your knees, as opposed to your heels.

3. Keep your spine in a neutral position. The back should not sag, nor should it hyperextend.

4. Allow the shoulders to soften away from your ears. Inhale, and imagine that the space between your vertebrae increases. Exhale; draw the abdominal muscle upward and inward, without moving your spine. Don't confuse this with the traditional "cat" exercise, where your back actually rounds.

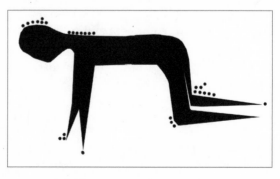

Remaining on all fours, you are now ready for the tripod balance.

Figure 1: Four-Point Drawing-in Maneuver

Tripod Balance

As you inhale in preparation, feel your spine elongate, and once again, allow your shoulders to slide away from the ears. As you exhale, draw the navel to your spine, as if your belly button was the ignition button that powers up the movement. Simultaneously extend your right leg and your left arm, keeping your left thumb facing upward. Try to remain centered rather than leaning into the opposite hip. Repeat on the opposite side. Make a mental note as to whether your balance is better on one side than the other. This will probably show up in your skiing. The tripod helps integrate the *multifidus,* the muscle close to your spinal column, with your deep core musculature. This is an excellent exercise to promote segmental spinal stability.

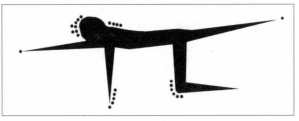

Figure 2: Tripod Balance

Postural Sway

Developing awareness of the body's natural amount of "sway" can help you tune-in to balance. Sway is constant in all movement, even when standing still. The nervous system generates unconscious, oscillating impulses to the muscles. These impulses help keep the body in an upright position. To experience this sensation, stand with your eyes closed, your feet parallel and about hip-width apart. Note the subtle fore/aft and side-to-side movement. Be aware of how your weight is transferred through your feet, and how this transference affects the rest of the body. Try this on one leg, then the other.

Fore/Aft Balance Exercise

Stand with one foot directly in front of the other, heel to toe. Arms are relaxed at your sides. Place all your weight on your rear foot, and then, gradually, transfer your weight to the front foot while keeping your torso stabilized. Do this about six times. Now perform these exercises while walking slowly, transferring your weight from heel to toe. Then walk slowly backward and feel the weight transfer from toe to heel. Take ten to twenty steps each way.

Proprioception Exercise

Stand on a piece of loose-leaf paper. Close your eyes, and march in place for one minute. Open your eyes.

Are you still on the paper?

POSTURE EXERCISES

The Pelvic Clock

The Pelvic Clock was created by an engineer named Moshe Feldenkrais. He believed that the body was a machine that could be programmed to perform with minimum effort but maximum efficiency. According to Feldenkrais, as early as infancy, your brain develops an image of how a movement should be performed. An incorrect image of a movement can cause you to perform in a manner that puts stress and strain on a joint while hindering efficiency.

As a result, he developed a series of exercises to help create new images for the brain. The program is called Awareness through Movement. If you re-read the chapter about the kinetic chain and the neurological basis for learning movement skills, you will see that this approach makes a good deal of sense.

While the Pelvic Clock is somewhat subtle, this sort of subtlety is needed to master the movements of alpine skiing. Don't worry if you need to read the instructions a few times before trying this exercise.

1. Your first step is to visualize your pelvis as a clock.

2. Lie on your back with knees bent and feet shoulder-width apart.

3. At 12:00, your abdominal muscles are drawn in as you roll your hipbones in the direction of your head in order to flatten your lower back into the mat.

4. At 6:00, you drop your hips and put more weight on the tailbone. Your back will be in a very slight arch.

5. At 3:00, the back of your left hip presses into the mat. There is a subtle lift of the right hip.

6. At 9:00, the right hip presses into the mat.

7. Once you have discovered the different positions, practice rotating the pelvis clockwise and counter-clockwise. Think about moving with fluidity. This is not a strip tease, so no bumping and grinding! In skiing and other snow sports, there are subtle changes in pelvic alignment as you edge from right to left or as your weight shifts forward and back. An overly dramatic pelvic movement can throw you off balance.

Heel Slides

This exercise can release the hip flexors while helping you practice the elusive parallel alignment needed for skiing. To avoid friction, you'll need to wear socks. Be sure that you have a smooth surface to slide along.

1. Lie on your back. Knees are bent; feet are flat and parallel on the floor. Try to keep your spine in a neutral position, which would imply a tiny curve at its base. You do not want to force your lower back into the floor for this exercise; doing so would tighten the hips flexors, thus defeating one of the purposes of the exercise.

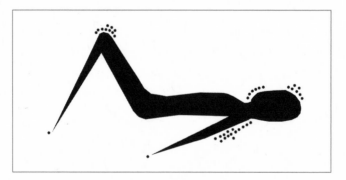

Figures 3. Heel slides, step 1

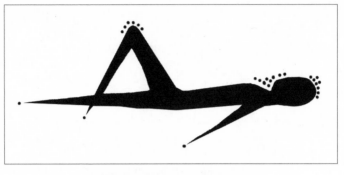

Figures 4. Heel slides, step 2

2. Inhale as you slide the heel of one foot along the floor, trying to maintain parallel alignment. Your lower back and your opposite leg should remain stable. Imagine that you are creating space between the hip flexor and pelvis.

3. Exhale as you slide the heel back toward your body.

4. Do four repetitions. With each repetition, imagine that your leg is becoming longer.

Modified Dead Bug

This exercise is derived from physical therapy. There are a multitude of variations, many of which involve performing the exercise with legs straight. Many people, though, have weak core muscles, as well as tight lower backs and hip flexors. If the deep core muscles do not have sufficient strength, performing this exercise with straight legs will cause the back to arch from the floor. This would defeat the purpose of the exercise while diminishing the effectiveness of its applications for skiing or other snow sports. We are looking for leg action that is devoid of excessive lumbar movement.

1. Lie on your back with your knees bent. Legs are held at what we call "table top" position. Calves are parallel to the floor; shins are parallel to the ceiling. Your spine should be pressed into the mat. Inhale in preparation. Feel as if you are sending your breath through your spine, allowing it to elongate into the floor.

2. As you exhale, draw your navel to your spine and lower one foot toward the floor, letting the toenails just barely touch the floor. Maintain your imprinted spine. Inhale and return to start.

3. Exhale and repeat on the other side.

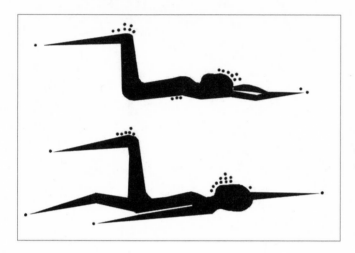

Figures 5 and 6. Modified Dead Bug

The Bridge

This exercise is a prerequisite for a more challenging one that will be done on the stability ball. Excellent alignment is needed to perform the more challenging version correctly. Working on the floor is a good place to start. Your goal in this exercise is to feel how the spine articulates. You also want to feel a connection between your deep core muscles and your spine.

1. Lie on your back. Knees are bent, feet flat and parallel.

2. Inhale to prepare

3. As you exhale, engage your core muscles and tilt the lower part of pelvis off of the floor. Imagine you are creating a hollow bowl from your navel to your pubic bone.

4. Inhale and return your lower pelvis to the floor.

5. Lift your pelvis, followed by your lower back.

6. Return your lower back to the floor, followed by your pelvis.

7. Lift your pelvis, lower back and middle back.

8. As you return, feel each vertebra articulate on the floor.

9. Lift your pelvis, lower back, middle back and upper back.

10.   When you return, make sure you let your lower back come down before your pelvis.

11.   Repeat eight times.

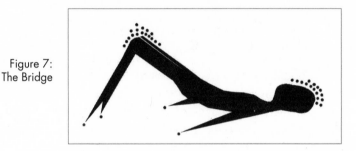

Figure 7:
The Bridge

Hip Turns

In most snow sports, especially skiing, upper/lower body separation is of paramount importance. Although there are more challenging ways to perform the following exercise, I have designed this variation to create a link between the actions of the feet and the deep core musculature. Throughout this exercise, your pinky toe and your belly button will lead you through the movements.

1. Lie on your back with your knees bent and your feet flat on the floor. Arms are extended, a little bit below shoulder level.

2. Inhale to prepare. Feel the back of the right shoulder blade sink into the mat.

3. As you exhale, try to feel as if your belly button is shifting to the left. Begin to tip your left pinky toe to the left. Your legs

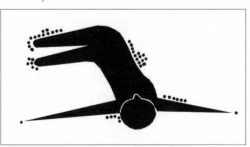

Figure 8. Hip Turns

will be angled to the left, with your weight on your left pinky toe and right big toe.

4. Inhale and hold this position for one second. Try to feel the back of your left shoulder blade sink deeper into the mat. Imagine that your have a curtain going across your chest.

5. To come back to center, exhale, and feel your belly button moving toward center. Simultaneously press your left big toe into the mat.

6. Repeat on the other side

Hip Turns with Medicine Ball

A variation on this exercise involves placing a small medicine ball between your inner thighs. Engaging your adductor (inner thigh) muscles helps activate your pelvic floor muscles. Additionally, having active adductor muscles can help prevent common ski injuries, such as the MCL tear.

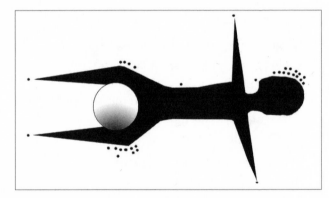

Figure 9.
Hip Turns with
Medicine Ball

Shoulder Movements

These upper-body exercises are of great benefit to skiers. Misalignment of the *scapula* will cause the *trapezius*, the muscles near the neck, to overwork. On the ski slope, this can cause sloppy pole plant, heightened sensitivity to cold (due to blocked circulation), and dysfunctional breathing. At the 2003 EpicSki Academy at Brighton, Utah, I conducted a series of postural alignments on some of the students. Many who had upper body misalignment were also told by their instructors that they had inaccurate pole plants.

Shoulder Shrugs

1. Lie on your back with your knees bent and feet parallel. Palms are flat on the floor facing downward, hands next to your hips.

2. As you inhale, slide your hands along the floor, elevating your shoulders upward toward your ears.

3. As you exhale, slide your shoulders downward. Here's an interesting image: Imagine you are sliding your armpits toward your waistline. You may feel a slight activation of your *latissimus dorsi*, which are the muscles that run laterally down the sides of your back.

4. Try it again. This time, as you release your shoulders, imagine that they are bars of soap sliding into your rear hip pockets. This will deactivate your *trapezius*, the muscles near your neck and upper shoulders, which are subject to extreme tension.

5. Try it once more. This time consciously increase the distance between the top of your shoulders and the tips of your ear lobes.

There. Isn't that better?

Scapular Stabilization

1. Lie on your back with your pinkies facing downward, thumbs upward.

2. Inhale in preparation.

3. As you exhale, imagine your belly button is the ignition button that powers all movement. Press your belly button inward; imagine your thumbs have helium balloons attached to them. Let your arms float toward the ceiling. Your head will stay on the floor.

4. As you inhale, imagine someone has strings on your pinkies. Then this nice person pulls on these strings, which causes the scapular—but not the head—to lift from the floor.

5. As you exhale, release back to neutral, keeping your fingers pointing toward the ceiling. This is called *scapular protraction*.

The opposite movement is called *scapular retraction*. Keep your hands and arms in the same position. Imagine you have a pencil between your shoulder blades. Squeeze your shoulder blades together to catch the pencil.

Now turn your palms downward. Allow your arms to float back to the start position. The back of the shoulders should be more into the floor than when you started and the shoulders should feel further away from your ears. Ahhhhhh!

Mentally record this sensation in your kinesthetic memory. This will be helpful on the slopes.

Plank with Hip Extension

1. Make a triangle with your elbows.

2 Curl your toes under.

3. Your torso should be on a straight line.

4. Inhale in preparation. As you exhale, contract your right glute and lift the leg off the ground, maintaining a neutral spine.

5. Inhale as you return.

6. Exhale as you repeat on the opposite side.

Do only as many repetitions as can be done in correct form. Keep your core muscles engaged, and do not allow your back to arch. Make sure that your neck and shoulders are relaxed. It helps to perform the shoulder shrugs and scapular stabilization exercises before you attempt the plank.

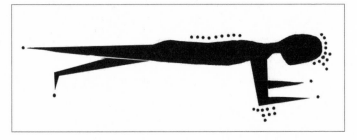

Figure 10: Plank with Hip Extension

Side-Lying Obliques

According to Warren Witherell, "the single most distinguishing trait of athletic skiers is the ability to ski in balance when their feet are far to one side of the body."

Lateral strength and stability is a crucial element of athletic skiing and other snow sports. In order to go way up your edges without toppling over, the external obliques need to be giving you some good lateral support.

Did you ever watch the way Bode Miller looks as if he's about to wipe out? But then he manages to bring himself back to center. This is due to exceptional lateral strength and stability. In a later chapter, we will attempt some extremely challenging external oblique exercises. But they are impossible to do without the proper alignment. The following is a good preparation exercise.

1. Lie on your right side.

2. Bend your right elbow, keeping it in alignment with your right shoulder.

3. Make sure that you are keeping all five fingers open.

4. Head should be aligned with the spine.

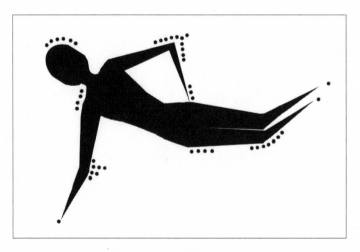

Figure 11. Side-Lying Obliques, position 1

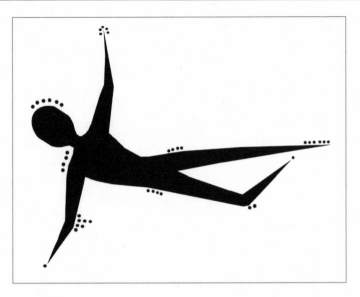

Figure 12. Side-Lying Obliques, position 2

5. Draw your navel to your spine. Inhale to prepare.

6. As you exhale, lift your right hip off the floor while straightening your left leg.

7. Hold for about five seconds.

8. Return.

9. Repeat for four more repetitions.

10. Change sides.

NINETEEN

Foot and Ankle Exercises

ANKLE ALPHABETS

Take off your shoes and sit on a chair. Draw the entire alphabet in cursive writing with one ankle, then the other.

TOE ARPEGGIO

Stay seated, with your feet flat on the floor. Begin with your big toe. Lift it off the floor, and let the others follow as if you were playing an arpeggio with your feet. Repeat on the other foot. You may find that it's easier on one side than the other. The next time you go skiing or snowboarding, see if there is a correlation.

ANKLE FLEXION

Dorsi flexion

Dorsi flexion occurs when we press the shin against the boot tongues. *Plantar flexion* happens when we lean back against the boot cuff. In some cases, skiers who have limited dorsi flexion will find themselves in the backseat on the skis, feeling a good deal of quadricep burn. Lack of dorsi flexion can often cause misalignment of the tibia. This in turn may effect the alignment of the femur. The integrity of the knee may become compromised.

As we get older, our range of motion in dorsi flexion diminishes. The Department of Physical Medicine and Rehabilitation at Chung-

Ho Memorial Hospital in Kaohsiung, Taiwan, performed a study where they discovered that dorsi flexion actually increased pelvic floor activity. As you may recall, the pelvic floor is responsible for stability, so this should be a good motivating factor for performing dorsi flexion exercises. If you would like to keep skiing or snowboarding long enough to finally get a senior citizen discount, practice dorsi flexion exercises at least once a week!

Dorsi Flexion Exercises

- Place your feet under a couch or table and lift up, pressing the top of your feet into the immovable object.

- Another excellent ski-specific way to work your dorsi flexors is to stand at the apex of an inclined step, such as the type that is used in step aerobics classes. Curl your toes toward your shins. You can also do this outdoors at the top of a hill.

The next exercise requires a stability ball and a theraband.

Ankle Flexion on the Ball

1. Sit on the ball with your legs facing a doorway.

2. Tie a loop at one end of a theraband.

3. Put your foot through the loop, keeping the band at the arch.

4. Tie a knot at the other end of the band.

5. Shut the knot in the door.

6. Move backward until the band feels taut.

7. Inhale to prepare.

8. Exhale as you pull your toes toward your face.

9. Perform ten repetitions with a straight leg and ten with a bent knee. Then switch legs.

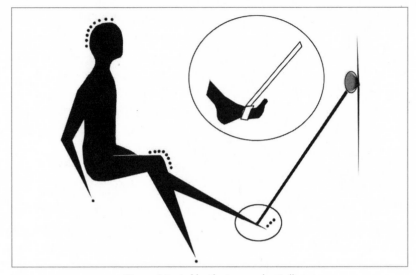

Figure 13: Ankle Flexion on the Ball

INVERSION AND EVERSION

Inversion and eversion are the movements of the ankle that assist in edge control.

Eversion

Sit facing a chair with your feet on the inside of the chair legs. Place your hands outside your knees for stabilization. Press against the chair legs with your feet.

Inversion

Sit facing a chair with your feet on the outside of the chair legs. Place your hands outside your knees for stabilization. Press against the chair legs with your feet.

Now that we've got you started on the right foot, let's play with a few balance toys.

TWENTY

Dynamic-Disc Exercises and Stability Ball Exercises

Many of the fundamental exercises from the previous chapters can be performed on the disc for added balance challenge.

DYNAMIC-DISC EXERCISES

Fore/Aft on the Dyna-disc

Since Dyna-Discs are inexpensive, many people get a few of them. You can set them up around the room and simply step from disc to disc. This challenges what we call your transitional balance, essentially balance in motion. If you get two discs, you can practice your edging skills. Try this:

Dyna-Disc Edging

1. Place the two discs next to each other

2. Place one foot one each disc

3. Keep your knees in a "soft" position

4. Shift your weight, so that you put pressure on the pinky toe of your left foot and the big toe of your right.

5. Come back to the neutral position.

Figure 14:
Fore/Aft on Dyna-Disc

6. Repeat in the opposite direction.

Perform a total of twenty repetitions.

You can also practice the tripod using two Dyna-Discs. This exercise will give you feedback as to whether you need to develop more stability in either your knees or your shoulder and scapula area.

Figure 15: Dyna-Disc Edging

Dyna-Disc Tripod

The Dyna-Discs can also be used to perform squats and lunges. You can even practice your balance skills while training your upper body. Stand on the discs as you perform shoulder, bicep, and tricep exercises. For knee stability, you can do a variation on the tripod exercise from chapter three. Place the disc under your non-moving knee. Engage your core muscles in order to minimize the wobble. When you've performed the exercise on both legs, place the disc under the non-moving hand. This will enhance scapular and shoulder stability, which are a crucial element of pole skills.

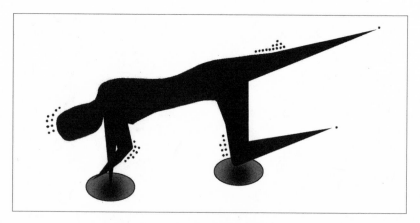

Figure 16: Dyna-Disc Tripods

The Dyna-Disc can also be used to practice one-legged balance exercises and mini squats. Mini-squats are great because they work the *vastus medialis,* the muscle responsible for the last ten degrees of extension. The smaller, fine motor movements of most snow sports rely on the use of the *vastus medialis.*

Figure 17:
Dyna-Disc Mini-Squats

Dyna-Disc Mini-Squats

1. Stand at the center of the disc.

2. Inhale to prepare.

3. Exhale as you lift one leg.

4. Inhale to prepare.

5. Exhale as you flex your standing leg.

6. Inhale as you straighten your leg.

7. Perform eight repetitions.

8. Change sides.

The following exercises use the rotating disc.

Rotations

Figure 18: Rotations

1. Place one disc under each foot.

2. Stand in an upright position.

3. Keep your knees soft, neither locked nor totally bent.

4. While maintaining a "quiet" upper body, rotate your feet from side to side.

5. Perform 50 repetitions.

A variation of the bridge exercise in the core-essential section can also be performed on the rotary discs.

Bridge with Rotation

1. Lie on your back.

2. Place each disc under each foot.

3. Extend your spine to the bridge position.

4. Rotate your feet from side to side, eight times.

5. Roll your spine back into the mat.

6. Perform six bridges with eight rotations on each bridge.

Keep in mind that although these exercises may be *helpful* for ski technique, having a pair of properly fitting boots is *essential* for efficient ski technique. If you enjoy the sport, it behooves you to see a good boot fitter.

STABILITY BALL EXERCISES

Start with a few basic exercises so that you can get used to the balance required for the more advanced ball exercises. Notice the difference in balance on one side as compared to the other. You might find that, coincidently, the same side has less balance on the hill.

Alternate Leg Balance

Seated on the stability ball, lift your left foot about one inch from the floor. Return, and then repeat on the other side. You can make this more challenging by performing this exercise with a medicine ball under your non-working foot.

Stability Medicine Ball Balance

1. Sit on your stability ball.

2. Place one foot on a medicine ball and the other on the floor.

3. Inhale to prepare.

4. As you exhale, lift your foot about one half inch from the floor.

5. Perform eight repetitions and change sides.

Once you've mastered this exercise, take the medicine ball out from under your foot. Begin to toss it from hand to hand. Once you have established a rhythm, as the ball reaches one hand, lift the corresponding foot about a half-inch from the floor.

Warning! This is not as easy as it sounds.

You can also perform the tripod on the stability ball.

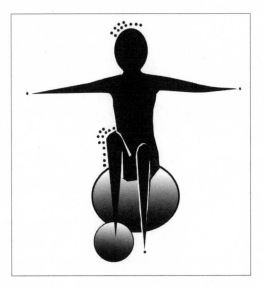

Figure 19:
Stability Medicine
Ball Balance

Tripod on the Stability Ball

1. Lie prone over the stability ball.

2. Inhale to prepare by pressing your hips firmly into the ball.

3. Exhale as you lift your right leg and leg arm.

4. Inhale as you press your left heel backwards, as if you were trying to get it to touch the floor.

5. Exhale as you roll the foot forward so that the top of the arch is on the floor.

6. Inhale as you return to center and lower the foot and arm.

Need a challenge? Perform this exercise with your feet on two Dyna-Discs!

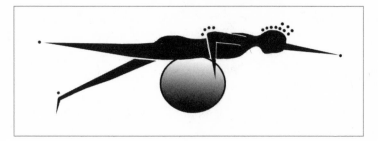

Figure 20: Stability Ball Tripod

Crossover

If you were to listen to a technical conversation among ski instructors, you might hear reference to the terms "crossover" and "cross-
under." In *The Complete Encyclopedia of Skiing,* Bob Barnes describes
how the center of mass moves from inside of one turn to the outside
of the next. Many skiers are reluctant to make this transference of
weight for fear of falling. As a result, they seem to be leaning uphill.
The turns become skids instead of glides.

Seated on the stability ball, take a big step to the right. Now bring
your left foot over to meet the right, feeling as if your belly button is
moving you in that direction. Repeat to the left. Now make the
moves bigger, so that you end up balanced on one cheek. Pretend
that your center is a small ball. You are "playing catch" with it as it
moves from one side of your body to the other.

When you feel comfortable, bring both feet as far to the right as
possible. Balance on your left cheek. Now let's practice edging. Roll
onto the pinky toe of your left foot and the big toe of your right foot.
Then flatten both feet. Repeat on the other side.

Bumping Bounces

Getting used to the bounce is an important part of bump skiing. In
order to stay on your skis, the core needs to be activated, and alignment must be optimal. Place your heels on the floor. Stabilize your
center, and begin bouncing.

Try a jumping jack. Use your inner thighs to bring you to center.
Engage your pelvic floor.

Go back to the crossover movement, adding this bounce. Feeling brave? Take this movement in a full circle around the ball. Is this too easy? Keep your feet together. First hop side to side, then do a full circle around the ball.

Mogul Skier

Keep the bounce. Angle knees to one side, while swinging your arms in the opposite direction.

Stability Ball Crunch

Inhale in preparation, sending the breath through the spine, creating a feeling of elongation. As you exhale, think of your belly button as the ignition button that powers the movement. Flex your torso. If you have neck trouble, rest your fingers lightly at the edge of your head.

1. Lie supine on the ball with your feet at a ninety-degree angle.

2. Inhale to prepare.

3. Exhale as you curl your rib cage toward your pelvis, while keeping your pelvis on the ball.

4. Inhale as you return.

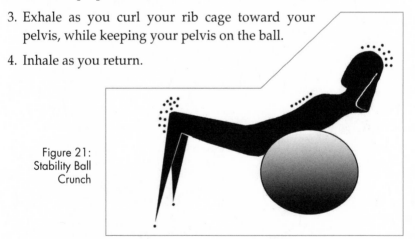

Figure 21:
Stability Ball
Crunch

Stability Ball Crunch and Toss

This variation of the stability ball crunch makes use of a medicine ball. Medicine balls weigh between two and five pounds. They are used to add resistance and agility training to your workouts. Given that you have to focus on the ball, they are also great tools for enhancing reaction time. You will need a partner, preferably of a similar height, for this exercise.

As a warm-up, sit facing your partner, and simply toss the ball back and forth to each other. Then each partner lifts one foot an inch from the floor. Continue to toss the ball. Then try the exercise while lifting the other foot. Try to maintain a stable upper body. Now let's make the balance more dynamic.

1. Partners sit facing each other on the ball, about one foot apart. One person sits upright.

2. The other holds the ball from the "crunch" position.

3. The person holding the ball tosses it to her partner. This brings her to the upright position.

4. As the partner catches the ball, she goes into the crunch position.

Only do as many repetitions as you can perform using good form. Stop if either partner feels the exercise in her neck or lower back.

Figure 22: Stability Ball Crunch and Toss, part 1

Figure 23:
Stability Ball Crunch
and Toss, part 2

Lateral Stability

According to Warren Witherall, "a single most distinguishing trait of athletic skiers is the ability to ski in balance when their feet are far to one side of their body." Lateral stability is essential for good skiing. If your goal is to carve your turns, angulation and inclination must occur. In *The Complete Encyclopedia of Skiing,* Bob Barnes defines angulation as a sideways bending of the joint, used to control edge angle. Angulation begins in the ankles, then follows through to the knees and hips.

Inclination is the act of leaning into the turn, offsetting the effects of centrifugal force. Angulation involves getting onto the edges of your skis, while inclination is the balance mechanism that allows for this movement.

Although the feet initiate angulation, the external obliques are responsible for enhancing the required lateral stability.

Stability Ball Side-Bend

1. Lie on your side with the stability ball under your waist and hips.

2. Extend your legs and anchor feet against a wall.

3. Cross your top leg in front of your bottom leg.

4. Bend your arms and place the hands by your ears. Drape your torso over the ball.

5. Inhale to prepare.

6. As you exhale, draw your navel toward your spine and lift torso in the opposite direction, bringing the side of the ribcage to the side of the hips. Don't let your pelvis roll forward or back on the ball.

7. Return to starting position and repeat for nine more repetitions.

8. Switch sides.

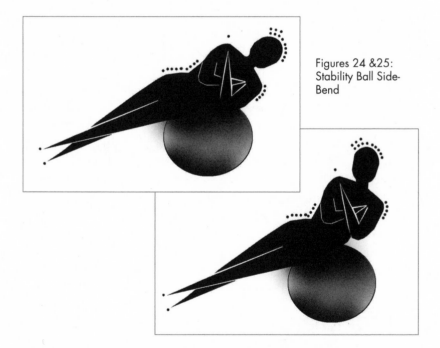

Figures 24 & 25: Stability Ball Side-Bend

Glute and Hamstring Stability Ball Exercises

This next group of exercises provides an excellent hamstring/gluteals workout, which in turn corrects muscular imbalances between the hamstrings and quadriceps. These muscles are crucial for injury prevention. Additionally, if you decide that you want to pursue mogul skiing, you need strong hamstrings to provide bump-proof stability.

Stability Ball Bridge

Review the bridge exercise featured in chapter five. Since you are now working on a piece of equipment that challenges your balance, good alignment and core activation is extremely important. The easiest way to learn this exercise is to drape your calves over the ball. Perform a few "bridges" to test your balance. Inhale to prepare, and then exhale as you extend upward to the bridge. The exhalation will help you engage your core muscles, which will in turn help with balance.

You can make the exercise slightly more challenging by placing a theraband across your lower pelvis. Hold the ends of the band firmly down to the floor. As you extend upwards into the bridge, you will be pressing against the resistance of the band. Perform eight repetitions.

On your last rep, stay up in the bridge. Now you are ready to "shoot the glute." As you inhale, lower your right glute cheek about three inches. Then, as you exhale, imagine that you can make a fist with your butt, and press the hip back to the starting position. Repeat on the other side. Perform sixteen repetitions, trying to establish an even rhythm as you work. Imagine that an elevator is traveling up the back of your legs, lifting your butt. To challenge your balance, as well as your hamstring, glute and core strength, perform the exercise with one leg draped on the ball while keeping the other bent knee on your chest.

1,000 Steps On The Ball

If you take ski lessons, you will one day take a class with an instructor who has you do a drill called the thousand steps. You can prepare yourself by trying it on the ball. The thousand steps is a drill that has the skier stepping from ski to ski throughout the entire turn. Ski instructors will tell you that the thousand steps develops balance, stance, mobility, edging skill, independent leg action as well as round turn shape. Since the thousand steps exercise requires continuous and dynamic activity, it is considered to be one of the best cures for the "static" skier.

Carefully extend the spine to the bridge. Engage your core, and do a little march on top of the ball. In case you were wondering, you do not have to do a thousand marches. Twenty is sufficient!

Balance discrepancies between the hamstrings and quadriceps are one factor that might make someone more susceptible to ACL injury. The stability ball hamstring curl is an excellent exercise for integrating dynamic hamstring strength with dynamic balance.

Stability Ball Hamstring Curl

1. Lie on your back with feet pelvic width apart. Toes are unclenched. The top of the head should be on the same line as the base of your spine. Hands should rest by your sides.

2. Inhale to prepare.

3. Exhale and extend your spine to the bridge.

4. Stay in the bridge. Inhale as you straighten your legs.

5. Remain in the bridge. Exhale as you bend your knees.

6. Keep your knees bent (no cheating!). Inhale as you return your spine to the mat.

At first, you will probably be able to do about four repetitions. Build up to eight. When you start to get stronger, perform the exercise with one leg.

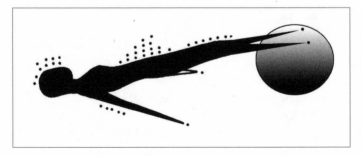

Figure 26: Stability Ball Hamstring Curl, part 1

Figure 27:
Stability Ball
Hamstring Curl,
part 2

One-legged Stability Ball Bridge

Figure 28:
One-Legged
Stability Ball
Bridge

Split Squat

The positioning in this exercise bears a slight resemblance to the stance used by telemarkers. Alpine skiers, though, can also derive benefit from it. Stand tall, placing one foot in front of the other. Place your rear foot on the stability ball. Make sure that the knee is facing downward, toward the floor. Your front foot should be facing straight ahead, like the headlight of a car. Shoulders should slide toward your rear hip pocket.

It is important to keep your head centered on your spine. Keep in mind that the head is the heaviest part of your body. And you thought it was your butt. Anyway, if it is misaligned, it may cause a domino effect, making your body tilt to one side. A centered head is a good habit to get into. On the slopes, ski instructors will tell you to focus down the hill. The body goes where the eyes lead. If you are looking in panic at the trees, you may end up there.

1. Inhale. Imagine that your breath goes up the vertebra of your spine, making you taller.

2. Exhale. Draw your belly button to your spine, flexing both knees.

3. Inhale, extend both legs, feeling as if your pelvic floor is drawing upward, like a hammock. Do not allow front knee to flex beyond the ankle.

4. Perform eight repetitions.

5. Switch sides.

This exercise also gives you excellent feedback as to whether your knees are tracking correctly. Tracking is important for directional control on the slopes.

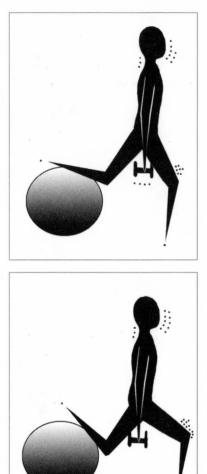

Figure 29 & 30: Split Squat

Side Hops

Stability-ball side hops are an excellent way to enhance athleticism. Place your hands on the stability ball, which will be lined up with your chest. Keep some weight in your arms. Squat down, and jump from side to side. Are we having fun yet?

Figure 31 & 32: Side Hops

Prone Knee Roll

The prone knee roll on the stability ball promotes excellent core strength. It is also a wonderful way to simulate the flexion and extension required for skiing. U.S. ski team exercise physiologist Scott Higgins considers flexion and extension of paramount importance. In his words, "world-class mogul courses require the ability of the athlete to extend and compress the body in concert with the shape of the snow. An important skill is to be able to move up and down through a long range of motion without balance changing in any way."

1. Assume a push-up position with your feet propped up on the stability ball and your hands resting on the floor under your shoulders, supporting your body weight.

2. Inhale to prepare.

3. As you exhale, hollow out your abdominal area and bend your knees, pulling them toward your chest and rolling the ball closer to your hands.

4. Inhale; engage your pelvic floor as you extend your knees to roll the ball out to the starting position.

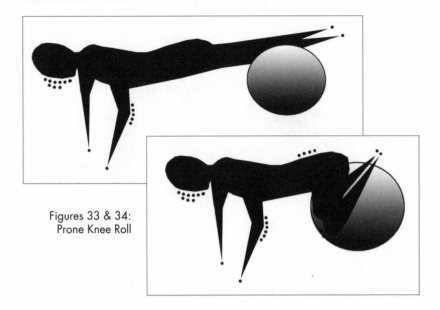

Figures 33 & 34:
Prone Knee Roll

Stability Ball Kneeling Roll-Out

Many people end up in what we call "the back seat" in skiing because they are afraid of the sensation of falling down the hill. This exercise can be helpful.

1. Kneel on the floor and place your forearms on the ball, making sure your hips and arms form a ninety-degree angle.

2. Inhale to prepare.

3. As you exhale, roll the ball forward as you extend your arms. Contract your abdominals to help support your lower back, which should not be strained. Your shins and calves will come off the floor. Roll as far forward as possible without compressing the spine, hunching the shoulders, or rounding the torso.

4. Inhale as you return.

If you have access to the seated slant board in the gym, you can make this even more ski-specific:

1. Stand behind the slant board, holding the stability ball with both hands.

2. Inhale to prepare.

3. Exhale; roll the ball down the slanted angle of the seated slant board.

4. Inhale to return.

5. Perform eight to twelve repetitions. When it starts to get to easy, try standing on a Dyna-Disc. On your last repetition, "edge" your feet from side to side while keeping the ball in a stable position.

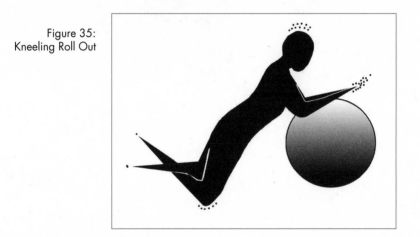

Figure 35:
Kneeling Roll Out

Stability Ball Reverse Curl

Warning! This is an extremely difficult exercise. It does, however, strengthen the lower core muscles while providing the pelvic flexibility needed for mogul skiing.

1. Place the stability ball next to the weight stack of the cable machine at the gym.

2. Hold on to the bar as shown in the picture.

3. Lift your feet off the floor.

4. Inhale to prepare

5. As you exhale, lift the lower part of your pelvis off the ball, as if you were doing a pelvic tilt.

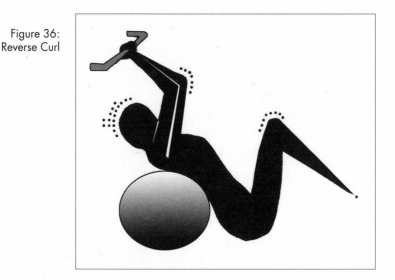

Figure 36:
Reverse Curl

While the stability ball is known for its versatility, standing with both feet on the ball is not recommended. The next chapter, however, on balance boards and the Bosu, features a variety of standing exercises.

TWENTY-ONE

Balance Board and Bosu Exercises

BALANCE BOARD EXERCISES

Balance Board Ankle Circles

For balance training, try making ankle circles while standing on a balance board. Start by shifting your weight from your toes to your heels. This is an important drill for snowboarders, who often talk about working from either the toe side or the heel side of the board. Now shift from side to side. This is an excellent exercise for skiers. Gradually work your way into a complete ankle circle. Keep a quiet upper body as you perform this exercise.

Figure 39: Ankle Circles

Pelvic Clock

Yes, this is the same one we tried on the floor and on the ball. Now we are using it dynamically. Remember that the movement is subtle. As you make the small circle with your hips, the board will also circle.

Weighting And Un-weighting

Stand on the board with your feet in parallel alignment, framing the Core Board logo. Begin to shift your weight from side to side. Be aware of the transference of weight from the pinky toe of one foot, to the big toe of the other foot. Try to initiate the movement in your feet rather than your hips.

One-Legged Balance Board Drills

One Legged Skiing and One-Legged Balance Board

Advanced skiing often requires one-legged balance skills. You can practice these skills on any sort of balance board.

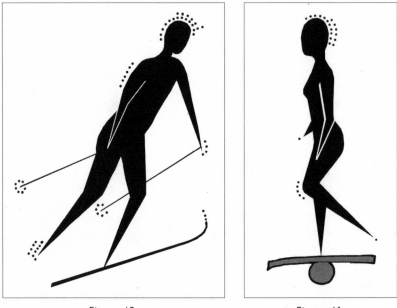

Figure 40:
One-Legged Skiing

Figure 41:
One-Legged Balance Board

Lateral Leaps

Start the weight/un-weight sequence described above. Then leap from one side to the other. Don't let the board bottom out.

Squats

Move to the front of the board. Perform six squats. Now do another six at the rear of the board. Then perform six squats at the right side and six squats on the left. Come to the center of the board, framing the logo. Perform another four squats. Hold the last squat in a tucked position. Shift your weight forward and back, then side to side. Remember; initiate the movement in your feet, not your hips. Once you have developed balance board confidence, you can try adding resistance. The Resources in the back of the book lists companies that sell bands that can be attached to a stable object. On the following pages are some examples of how resistance can be applied while performing squats on a balance board.

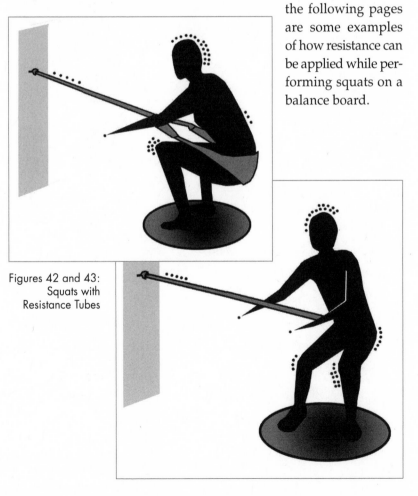

Figures 42 and 43: Squats with Resistance Tubes

Running Squats

Hold your squat position at the center of the board. Keep your feet completely flat on the board. Do a sprinting action of the feet, but keep your knees bent. Do not let the board bottom out.

Squats with Resistance Tubes

Lateral balance and external oblique strength can also be improved by using either a small medicine ball or a five-pound weight.

Skier's Image

Look at the angulation in figure 43, and compare it to the angulation in figure 44. As you perform this exercise keep this image in your mind's eye.

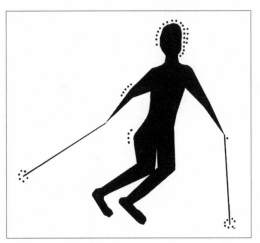

Figure 44:
Skier's Image

Balance Board Side Bend

1. Stand at the center of the board.

2. Hold a medicine ball or a five-pound weight in one hand.

3. Inhale to prepare.

4. As you exhale, engage your core and bend at the waist to the right.

5. Inhale as you return to center.

6. Perform eight to twelve repetitions.

7. Switch sides.

Although the board will obviously move, try not to let it touch the ground.

You've played with the balls. You've played with the boards. Now let's look at life from both sides as we explore the Bosu.

BOSU EXERCISES

When exercising on the Bosu, it is important to wear supportive footwear for plyometric moves. For ankle strength, however, and to enhance proprioception, try working barefoot.

Proprioception

Start by simply standing on the Bosu. Now close your eyes. You will probably feel an exaggeration of the body's mechanisms for adjusting to balance challenges. Open your eyes and raise one arm. Follow it with your eyes. Keep following your hand as you bring it down, to the left and right, and back behind you. Repeat this using your opposite arm.

Fore/Aft Balance

Stand at the center of the dome. Shift your weight forward and back, going from plantar flexion to dorsi flexion. Now stand in front of the bull's eye, so that you are going "downhill." Shift your weight toward your toes into plantar flexion, and then back to neutral. Then stand behind the bull's eye. Shift your weight from dorsi flexion to neutral.

Compressions

Stand on top of the dome side of the Bosu. Perform a pedaling action of the feet. You can do this throughout the workout, anytime that you feel your feet cramping up. Build the compressions into a march, then into a jog.

Lateral Balance

Perform edging movements by shifting weight onto the big toe of the left foot and the pinky toe of the right. Reverse directions. Then stand slightly to the right of the bull's eye. Shift your weight toward the right pinky toe, and then back to neutral. Repeat on the left side of the bull's eye, shifting toward your left pinky toe.

Bosu Carver

1. Stand on top of the Bosu.

2. Shift your weight so that you are on the pinky toe of the left foot and big toe of the right.

3. Shift to the other side.

4. Engage your core muscles to keep a quiet upper body.

Figure 45: Bosu Carver

Full Squats

Try going into a full squat. Your knees should face straight ahead, like the headlights of a car. On your last repetition, hold the squat. For snowboarding, shift your weight from your heels to your toes. Skiers should practice the carving movements that were performed in the upright position.

Bosu Leg Balances

Once again, make sure that the toes of the supporting foot are unclenched and the knee is kept in parallel alignment.

Advanced Exercises: Proceed with Caution!

One-Legged Mini-Squats

1. Stand, balancing on your left leg.

2. Inhale to prepare.

3. Exhale as you bend your left knee.

4. Inhale to straighten.

5. Perform twelve repetitions.

6. Switch legs.

Perform three sets for each leg.

Jump And Stick

1. Stand on top of the Bosu. Feet are parallel, and open to the width of your average ski stance.

2. Inhale and jump.

3. As you exhale, land in this sequence: Toes first, then the ball of the foot, then the heels, then squat. If your body is in correct alignment, there will be minimal wobbling of the feet upon landing. Don't expect, though, to be paralyzed. Remember, athletic balance is dynamic. There may be some small degree of motion occurring.

Squat Jump with Medicine Ball

You can add agility training to the above exercise by tossing a medicine ball in the air as you jump up, and catching it when you land in the squat.

Figure 46 & 47: Squat Jump with Medicine Ball

Freestyle Skier

No snow, no prob-
lem. Ski in the the-
atre of your mind as
you perform the Bosu
Jump series.

Figure 48:
Freestyle Skier

Bosu Bridges

The bridge we learned in core-essentials turned out to be a useful skill. Here is a version you can perform on the Bosu.

1. Turn the Bosu platform-side up.

2. Lie on your back, placing your feet hip width apart at the center of the Bosu.

3. Inhale to prepare.

4. Exhale as you extend your spine to a bridge.

5. At the top, inhale in preparation.

6. Exhale as you rock the Bosu forward.

7. Inhale back to center.

8. Exhale and rock it back.

9. Inhale back to center.

10. Perform eight repetitions.

11. Exhale and roll down your spine, vertebra by vertebra.

12. Perform two more sets.

Lateral Plyometric Jumps

Some studies have shown that practicing plyometrics can actually prevent knee injuries. This next exercise, though, should only be performed if you are injury-free.

1. Stand to the left of the Bosu.

2. Place your right foot on the Bosu. Toes point straight ahead.

3. Place your left foot on the floor. Toes of the left foot should be on the same line as the right.

4. Squat.

5. In an explosive movement, inhale, extend both legs, bringing both feet on to the Bosu.

6. Exhale, land in a squat on the right side of the Bosu.

Figure 49:
Lateral
Plyometric
Jumps

Figure 50: Jump Turns

Jump Turns

Do you want to have some fun? Try a quarter-turn in each direction. Then try a 180-degree turn. If you are feeling spunky, try a 360-degree turn. Snowboarders and freestyle skiers love them.

Hint: Pick a visual or image to "spot" as you turn.

Bosu Stability Ball Split Squat

Just in case the split-squat using the stability ball has become too easy, you can do the same exercise with your standing leg on the Bosu.

Figure 51: Bosu Stability Ball Split Squat

Bosu Partner Upper-Body Training

If you have a training partner, you can also perform some upper-body conditioning while training you balance skills.

1. Partners face each other on the Bosu.

2. Each partner holds one end of a resistance band in her right hand.

3. Inhale to prepare.

4. As you both exhale, one partner performs a one-arm row while the other extends his arm and performs a squat.

5. Inhale as you return to center.

6. Perform eight to twelve repetitions.

7. Switch sides.

When you have completed both arms, partners should switch roles.

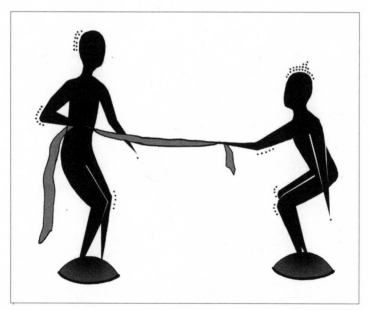

Figure 52: Bosu Partner Upper-Body Training

Bosu Obliques

Mogul skiing requires strong obliques, and a good sense of upper and lower body separation. To prepare for this extremely challenging exercise, practice the hip turns with medicine ball featured in chapter five.

Figure 53: Bosu Obliques

1. Sit at the apex of the Bosu.

2. Inhale to prepare.

3. As you exhale, angle your feet very slightly to the right, and let your torso turn slightly to the left.

4. Inhale as you return to center.

5. Switch sides.

Upper/Lower Body Separation

When you have gained a significant amount of skill in both the Bosu jump and Bosu oblique series, you can practice jumps that teach the upper/lower body separation that is required for good skiing.

1. Stand on top of the Bosu.

2. Make sure that your toes are unclenched.

3. Keep your upper body facing down an imaginary fall line.

4. As you jump, turn your hips and feet to the left, without turning your upper body.

5. Return to center.

6. Repeat on the right.

To avoid turning your upper body, get a clear visualization of the slope in front of you. Imagine the other skiers and riders that you need to watch out for.

TWENTY-TWO

Resistance Band and Sliding Board Exercises

ELASTIC RESISTANCE EXERCISES

Tuck Squats

The tuck squat uses muscle groups that are similar to those that racers use in a skier's tuck position.

1. Sit in a low chair, with a resistance band under your feet.

2. Bring the handles of the band up to your shoulders.

3. Inhale and lift your butt about two inches off the chair.

4. Exhale as you lower your butt about an inch. Don't let your butt touch the chair.

5. Perform three sets of twelve repetitions.

When you get good at this, try it on one leg. Remember, for this particular exercise, you will never completely straighten your legs.

Lateral Resistance Hops

You will need an extremely strong tube for this exercise, as well as a door attachment. Some companies make a specific belt that attaches to the band for this purpose.

1. Attach the tube to the door.

2. Stand sideways with your right hip facing the door.

3. Step away from the door until there is no slack.

4. Jump from side to side.

Warning: Do not do the lateral jumping exercise if you have knee injuries (or nasty downstairs neighbors). Use only the strongest tubing available.

Band Walk

Attach the smaller band around your ankles.

Side-step, taking four steps to the right and then four steps to the left. Keep your feet parallel. Perform this exercise until you feel a burn in your outer thighs. Remember to keep your core muscles engaged and your

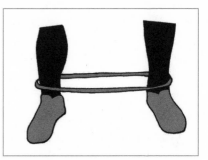

Figure 54: Band Walk

shoulders relaxed. You can also do this exercise in a squat position, keeping your knees bent the entire time.

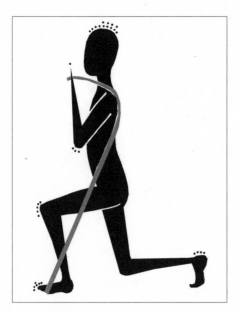

Band Lunges

Resistance bands can also be used to add challenge to squats and lunges.

Figure 55:
Band Lunges

TELEMARKERS

You can see why telemarkers love this exercise.

1. Place tubing or band under your left foot.

2. Bring the handles up to your shoulder.

3. Inhale to prepare.

4. As you exhale, bend both knees.

5. Inhale as you straighten your legs.

6. Perform twelve repetitions.

7. Change sides.

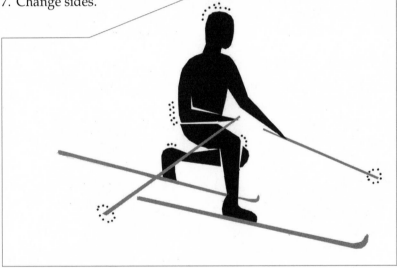

Figure 56: Telemarkers

Slide Board Exercises

Safe-Sliding Guidelines

Approach the board from the back. Balance is better when you are stepping forward onto a slick surface, rather than stepping backward. At first, the slide board can be rather challenging. You will want to spend a few moments warming up your muscles with smaller movements.

Slide Warm-up One

1. Stand at one end of the board, with your right foot placed firmly against the end ramp.

2. Keep your knees flexed and aligned over the middle of your feet. Do not allow your knees to extend beyond your toes.

3. As you inhale, slide your left foot away from your body

4. As you exhale, tighten your inner thigh muscle and draw the leg back in towards the ramp.

Perform eight repetitions, and then turn so that you are facing the ramp.

Slide Warm-up Two

Stand facing the ramp. Place your right foot on the ramp and your left foot on the slide board.

1. Inhale to prepare

2. Exhale and slide your left foot along the board till you end up in a lunge. Your right knee will be bent, and your left leg will be straight. Keep your heel in constant contact with the slide board.

3. Inhale and slide the leg back to the ramp.

4. Perform eight repetitions on each leg, and then turn back to the original position, facing straight ahead.

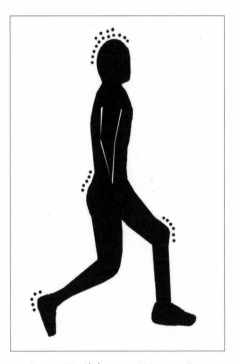

Figure 57: Slide Lunge Warm-up Two

Slide Jacks

The next exercise prepares you to slide across the board. Slide your left foot out. Slide your right foot in to meet it. Take as many steps as you need to get you to the other side. Then, repeat the sequence on the other leg. Guess what? If you are a skier, you can use this sequence to warm up on snow. It can be performed in either your boots are with skis!

Now you are ready to go across the board. Face straight ahead, with your right foot on the ramp and your left foot on the slide board. Inhale to prepare, and then, as you exhale, try to slide across the board. A few pointers

- As you push off, keep a low body position.

- Although you are pushing with your foot, try to consciously activate your gluteals and outer thigh muscles.

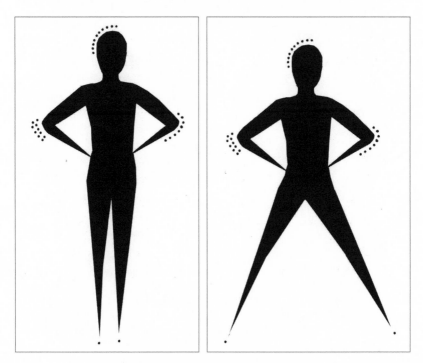

Figure 58 &59 Slide Jacks Step 1 and Step 2

- Keep your shoulders in alignment with your hips
- Challenge yourself by working in a squat position.

Do not be concerned if at first you cannot get all the way across the board. Go halfway across and then side step back. Eventually, your adductors, or inner thigh muscles will get stronger, and you will make it to the other side. I promise! Once you become really advanced, you can stand in the middle of the board and perform slide jumping jacks. These are essentially the same thing as a regular jumping jack, but your feet stay on the slide board.

Cross-country skiers enjoy doing a variation of the lunge warm-up in the middle of the board. Instead of sliding back with one leg at a time, keep alternating legs as if you were cross-country skiing.

If a slide board isn't in your budget, but you have access to a wooden floor, you can devise a makeshift slide with a hand towel. Place the towel under one foot and glide out and in. You can also try this with heavy socks after you have waxed your floors. Another product, the Gliding Disc, comes with a set of two discs. You can choose discs for either a wooden floor or for use on a carpet.

TWENTY-THREE

Integrated Training Exercises

LOWER BODY INTEGRATED STRENGTH SEQUENCES

Squat Rack

1. Perform one or two sets of eight to twelve repetitions on the squat rack.

2. For the next two sets of eight repetitions, perform two one-legged ball squats.

3. Place your right foot on the stability ball.

4. Inhale to prepare.

5. Exhale as you come down into the squat, straightening your right leg so that it extends directly in front of the body. Watch the tracking of your knees.

6. Inhale as you bend your knee to return.

Perform twelve repetitions and then repeat the exercise on the other leg.

Leg Press

Now for something completely different. After performing one or two sets of eight to twelve repetitions on the leg press, head over to the pull-up machine, usually used for upper body work. Take a

Dyna-Disc with you. Set the weight as if you were doing a leg exercise, not an upper body exercise. Place a Dyna-Disc on the kneepad. Put one foot on the step, and your working foot on the disc that is on the pad. Hold on to the upper bars.

1. Inhale to prepare.

2. Exhale as you press down on the pad to straighten your leg.

3. Inhale to bend it.

4. Perform twelve repetitions, and then switch sides.

Hamstring Curl

Perform two sets of eight to twelve repetitions on the leg curl.

Stability Ball Dead Lift

For the next two sets of eight repetitions, try the stability ball dead lift

1. Stand with one foot on the ball.

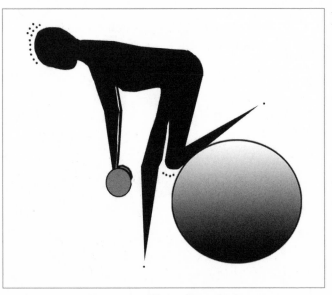

Figure 59: Stability Ball Dead Lift

2. Keep your standing leg slightly bent.

3. Dumbbells are in front of your thighs.

4. Keep your shoulders relaxed, your spine elongated and core muscles engaged.

5. Inhale to prepare

6. Exhale as you tip from the hips and bring weights down to knees, keeping your hands close to thighs.

7. Inhale as you contract your glutes and hamstrings to pull your torso back up.

Abductor Machine

Perform two sets of eight to twelve repetitions on the abductor machine.

Stability Ball Leg Raise

For the next exercise and a few of the others, you will need the Balance Ball Resistance Kit, an inexpensive series of straps that fit over your ball, providing two resistance bands for strength training. Having the bands attached to the ball allows for a wide variety of upper and lower body exercises while eliminating the need for door attachments that are sometimes necessary for band work.

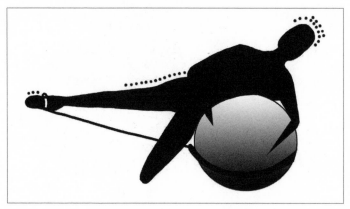

Figure 61: Stability Ball Leg Raise

1. Lie sideways on the ball with one resistance band under the ball and coming out the side.

2. Place the top foot inside the handle and extend the leg.

3. Keep your shoulders over your hips and your upper body "quiet."

4. Inhale to prepare.

5. Exhale as you lift the top leg a few inches off the floor.

6. Inhale to return.

7. Perform eight to twelve repetitions.

8. Switch sides.

Now, perform two sets of 8-12 repetitions on the adductor machine. Then, try the adductor squeeze bridge.

Adductor Squeeze Bridge

The next exercise requires a Pilates fitness circle and a stability ball. The fitness circle is a ring constructed of sprung steel. When you

Figure 62: Adductor Squeeze Bridge

use the circle in conjunction with the stability ball bridge, you add an adductor workout to your glute and core training. Simply put your feet on the ball and place the circle between the inner thighs. Squeeze in as you come up into the bridge; relax the inner thighs as you descend.

UPPER BODY INTEGRATED STRENGTH SEQUENCES

Although the lower body is usually the primary focus of snow-sport specific workouts, it is advisable to include some upper-body conditioning. Snow-sport equipment is heavy. If you are exhausted after carrying your skis and boots from the parking lot, your skiing will be less enjoyable. And don't forget about the occasional polling on the flatter slopes. You will be glad that you worked out your triceps! If you are a Nordic skier, nobody needs to convince you about the importance of upper body strength.

Even more important, is the effect of upper body training on postural alignment. Many gym rats put far too much emphasis on the pectorals. Then they go back to work, and sit hunched over a computer, exacerbating faulty alignment. Strengthening the *latissimus dorsi* and rhomboids may correct this muscle imbalance.

Upper Back Exercises

Perform three sets of twelve repetitions on a rowing machine. Then grab a stability ball and a dumbbell for the stability ball row.

Stability Ball Row

1. Place your left foot on the ball.

2. Hold a dumbbell with your left hand.

3. Inhale to prepare.

4. As you exhale, contract your left shoulder blade and perform a row.

5. Do eight repetitions.

6. Switch sides.

Figure 62: Stability Ball Row

Front Deltoids

Begin by performing two sets of front deltoid raises. Then set up a resistance tube using one of the devices that attach it to a stable object and take out the balance board. Place the board in front of the object to which the tubing is attached. Your back will be facing the stable object.

Grab one tube handle in each hand. Your thumbs should face upward and your pinkies face down, as if you were holding ski poles. Inhale to prepare. As you exhale, perform a squat, while you simultaneously raise both arms to shoulder height. The board will rock forward. Pretend that you are skiing down a slope. Inhale as you lower your arms and return to an upright position.

Biceps

Perform two sets of bicep curls. Then set up the stability ball resistance kit for the bicep curl bridge.

Stability Ball Bicep Bridge

1. Lie on your back with your feet on the ball.

2. Hold one handle in each hand.

3. Inhale to prepare.

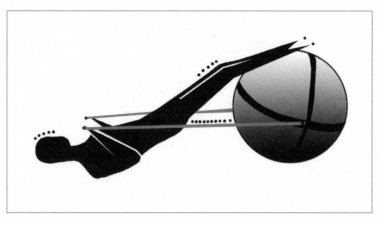

Figure 64: Stability Ball Tricep Bridge

4. As you exhale, simultaneously perform a bicep curl and a bridge, without letting your elbows leave the floor.

5. Inhale to return.

Triceps

After performing two or three sets of trip extensions, you are ready for tricep dips on the ball. This challenging exercise also promotes scapula stability.

Stability Ball Tricep Dip

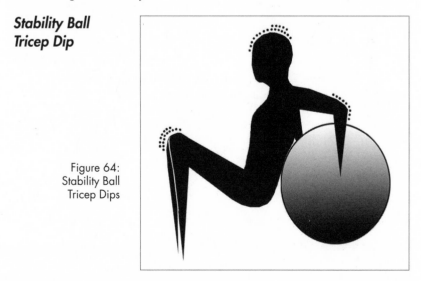

Figure 64:
Stability Ball
Tricep Dips

INTEGRATED PLYOMETRIC TRAINING: JUMPING FOR JOY

In Part One, we talked about the different types of muscle contractions, and how you can literally jump for joy while training. Here are some exercises to try. You might want to review the information in chapter ten to make sure you're using the proper technique.

The following exercises should be preceded by a traditional set of leg presses, squats or lunges.

Jump/Reach

This exercise involves the integration of core, leg and hip strength. Begin in a partial squat, Follow it be a quick jump forward. Aim for height, as opposed to repetition. Remember to land quietly, sequencing the landing as toe ball heel squat.

Jump/Tuck

Begin in a squat, then jump up explosively. Bring your knees to your chest. Imagine that you are catching big air.

Twist/Jump

Begin by standing in a neutral position. As you jump up quickly swivel your hips in one direction. Land in neutral, then repeat, twisting the other way.

Lunge Jump

Drop down into a lunge. Jump up, reaching for the ceiling. Scissor your legs in mid-air. Repeat on the other side.

TWENTY-FOUR

Agility Training

THE SKI-AGILITY WORKOUT

Try this drill. Have a friend help you out. Begin a jog. Gradually, pick up your speed. At any point, have your friend yell, "Stop!" Now check your alignment. To decelerate safely, your weight needs to be forward. The ball of the foot should be firmly planted on the ground, and both of your knees should be bent.

There are many other ways to train for agility in the off-season. Jumping rope will develop fast feet. Inline skating can help develop some ski-specific skills. If you skate in an urban area, you will certainly be improving your reaction time.

JUMPING THROUGH HOOPS

Although many athletic companies sell an expensive device called an agility ladder, you can devise an economical version of this tool by purchasing a

Figure 65: Jumping Through Hoops

bunch of hoola-hoops. Set them up in a room, and hop from hoop to hoop. In the warmer season, take the hoops to an outdoor hill. Practice hopping both uphill and downhill. This is also an excellent exercise for developing strategy for skiing moguls.

HAVE A BALL WITH A BUDDY

You can also create an agility course by arranging a variety of balance toys such as a Bosu, Dyna-Discs and a wobble board in a pattern, and walking from one piece of equipment to another. Practicing with a friend is always more fun. Each of you can stand on a different balance device and play a game of catch.

Speaking of friends, the next exercise combines strength, one-legged balance and agility in one great exercise. The element of agility comes from the fact that you need to sense your partner's movements and rhythms and adjust your own accordingly. So grab a partner, and let's get started.

Figure 66: Have a Ball with a Buddy

1. Stand side-by-side with your partner, placing a stability ball between your hips.

2. Lift your inside foot from the floor.

3. Inhale to prepare.

4. As you exhale, perform a mini-squat with your outside leg.

5. Inhale as you straighten your leg.

6. Perform twelve repetitions

7. Switch sides.

Were you able to sense the rhythm of your partner's movements? This sort of sensitivity is paramount on the slopes, where terrain conditions can change at a moment's notice. In fact, sensitivity and awareness are the prerequisites for agility. Once you develop this ability to tune in to other people as well the conditions in your environment, you just might find that it can carry over into new hobbies.

TWENTY-FIVE

Dynamic Flexibility and Foam Roller Stretches

STABILITY BALL HIP CIRCLE

If you deflate your stability ball and bring along a small pump, there are some warm-up exercises you can perform. Try the stability ball hip circle:

1. Sit on the ball with your knees bent at a 90-degree angle.

2. Inhale to prepare.

3. Exhale as you circle your hips to the left.

4. Inhale as you return to center.

5. Exhale as you circle to the right.

6. Inhale as you return.

7. Keep a "quiet" upper body.

8. Sit tall! Rather than resting your hands on your thighs, which promotes slouching, rest your hand on the ball.

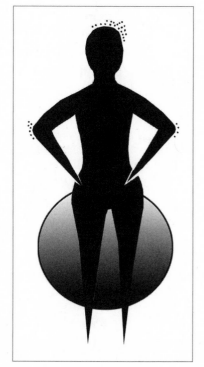

Figure 67:
Stability Ball Hip Circle

There are a number of great ways to warm up for snow sports. In the lodge, practice just a few of the basic balance exercises and the postural alignment exercises in chapter eighteen, and the foot-and-ankle exercises in chapter nineteen. Additionally, some of the sliding and gliding exercises can actually be performed on the snow.

PUTTING THE "AH" INTO APRÈS SKI

Static stretching does have its place. At the end of a hard day on the slopes, nothing feels better than a good stretching session. The hot tub also feels great, and it gives you a chance to socialize and commiserate with your fellow snow-sport enthusiasts. If you are single, many a romance (both torrid and everlasting) has begun in a ski area hot tub. A massage is also great if you can afford it.

If you want to combine the benefits of stretching and massage, consider investing in a foam roller. These products have been making a big hit in the sports-training market. Foam roller flexibility training is known as *myofascial self-release*. It helps you release muscular tension without significantly altering muscle length. Since muscle length is not affected, foam roller flexibility exercises can even be used to release tension prior to winter sport activity. Here are some important guidelines for foam roller flexibility exercises:

• Holding each position one to two minutes for each side.

• Stop rolling and rest on the painful areas for twenty to thirty seconds if you feel intense pain on any particular area.

• Continuing to roll when pain is present activates the muscle spindles, which will create increased tightness and pain.

• Resting twenty to thirty seconds on painful areas will inhibit the muscle spindles, which in turn will reduce muscular tension and pain.

FOAM ROLLER EXERCISES

Foam roller exercises can be performed for every part of the body. The following foam roller stretches will feel great after a day on the slopes.

The Illio-Tibial Band Foam Roller IT Stretch

1. Set this up like the side of calf roll, but start on the hip.

2. Roll from knee to hip; slowly roll to find "hot spots." Believe me, you will.

3. Stack legs or drop your right foot to the ground.

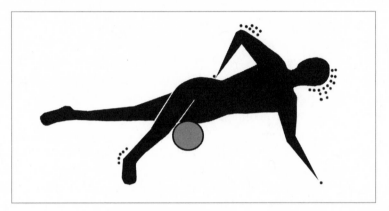

Figure 68: IT Stretch

Quadricpes Foam Roller Stretch

1. Balance on your elbows; face down, with quads on foam roller.

2. Work your way up the roller, while engaging your core.

3. To place greater emphasis on one leg, cross one leg over the other.

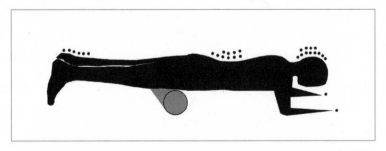

Figure 69: Foam Roller Stretch

BODY ROLLING: ROLLING WITH THE PUNCHES

If you're looking for a portable device that can be used to release tension and increase dynamic flexibility, consider Body Rolling. This fantastic technique is similar to foam-roller release. When going on a snow-sliding vacation, though, a ball is far more portable than a roller. Body Rolling works in the same way a massage therapist would work. Body Rolling creator Yamuna Zake, though, believes that people should have self-empowerment when it comes to their health. She created this technique as a means of providing affordable "massage therapy" that can be self-administered at any time.

The Body Rolling ball replaces the massage therapist's hands as it moves on muscles to increase blood flow and promote healing. The Body Rolling Foot Walkers have a similar surface to the Dyna-Discs. They are shaped to conform, though, to the arches of your feet. The plastic half-spheres are covered with knobbles that stimulate the bottom of the foot, thereby increasing circulation. Skiers, whose boots are less comfortable than those of other snow sliders, will love using these at the end of a day on the slopes.

Body Rolling Foot Stretch

Stand with your toes on the floor, and your feet draped over the sphere. Breathe deeply, and allow the weight of your body to sink into the sphere. You can also do this exercise by standing behind the Foot Walkers, placing your heels on the floor and the soles of your feet over the sphere. This helps enhance dorsi flexion, crucial for downhill skiers.

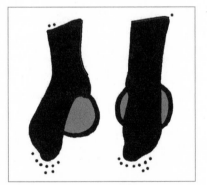

Figure 70: Foot Stretch

AFTERTHOUGHT

Finiation

I once had a ski instructor who liked to talk about the "Finitiation" of a turn. Finitiation refers to the fluid transition between the completion of one turn into the initiation of the next one. As I come to the completion of this book, I realize that I am initiating a new phase of my life by becoming a published author.

Yet looking back on my life, I can see that every initiative I took enticed me to follow the trail that eventually lead to where I am today. After working as a children's movement counselor at a day camp, I joined a small gym near my home. I still remember the name: *Elaine Powers Figure Salon*. Does anyone even use the word "figure" anymore? Ten months later, I used my credentials as a movement counselor to get a job as an "exercise instructor," another outdated term. Then, against my parents' wishes, I got a job handing out circulars for a men's health club. A few months later, the manager of that club opened a coed gym and hired me as an instructor. The rest is history. The end of each employment experience became the beginning of a new one.

So what's next? Who knows? Acting is reacting!

Bibliography & References

Barnes, Bob. *The Complete Encyclopedia of Skiing:* Silverthorne, CO: Snowline Press, 1992.

Clark, Michael, Corn Rodney. *Optimum Performance Training for the Fitness Professional:* Calabasas, CA: National Academy of Sports Medicine, 2001.

Cook, Gray. *Athletic Body in Balance.* Champaign, IL: Human Kinetics, 2003.

Crowley, Chris, and Henry Lodge, M.D. *Younger Next Year for Women.* New York, NY: Workman Publishing Company, 2005

Crum, Thomas F. *Journey to Center: Lessons in Unifying Body, Mind, and Spirit.* New York: Fireside, 1997.

Ettinger, Carl. vermontskisafety.com

Foley, Kevin. At Home in the Discomfort Zone Outside Online, April 2002

Gambetta, Vern. *Too Loose Too Much* at tinyurl.com/j9yx6 or gambetta. com/noticia.php?id=10&SesID=fc31a937151312b510cdbcfddbd4a2dc, accessed August 2006.

Hodges, P.W., and C.A. Richardson, "Inefficient muscular stabilization of the lumbar spine associated with low back pain: a motor control evaluation of *transversus abdominis*." *Spine* 21:2640–50; 1996.

Houston, Charles. *Going Higher: Oxygen, Man and Mountain.* Seattle, WA: Mountaineers Books, 1998.

Lachapelle, Delores. *Deep Powder Snow: Forty-Years of Ecstatic Skiing, Avalanches, and Earth Wisdom.* Durango, CO: Kivak Press, 1992.

Markova, Dawna. *I Will Not Die an Unlived Life.* San Francisco, CA: Conari Press, 2000.

Oprah.com: "Virginia Madsen's Aha Moment" *Oprah Magazine,* January, 2006.

Seiller, Barry, M.D.: "See Strong to Ski Strong," Visual Fitness Institute article at VisualFitness.com, 1999.

Weck, David. *Bosu Early Adaptors, Creativity and Influence* bosufitness.com/blog/2006/03/dw/bosu-early-adopters-creativity-influence.

Westfeldt, Weems. *Brilliant Skiing.* Aspen, CO: Aspen Skiing Company, 2006.

Glossary

Snow Sport Terms

Backcountry skiing or snowboarding: Backcountry skiing or off-piste skiing is skiing in a sparsely inhabited rural region, where fixed mechanical means of ascent (chairlifts, cable cars etc.) are not present.

Bump: Mounds in a ski slope formed when skiers cut grooves in the snow as they execute turns. Also known as moguls.

Bump run: Also known as mogul fields, are formed when skiers or snowboarders cut grooves in the snow while executing turns. In addition, some areas of the mountain feature bumps that are purposely built in order to create a more challenging skiing or snowboarding experience. Bump runs require an enormous amount of agility, balance, skill and strength.

Carving: Making turns on the ski or snowboard with the edges cutting into the hill.

Cross-Country Skiing: Skiing without the use of chair lifts. Also known as Nordic Skiing. Can be performed on specially designed cross country tracks, or in the backcountry.

Cruising: Making a long run down the slopes at a relaxed pace.

Din setting: A din setting refers to the Deutsche Industrie Normen. It is an internationally agreed scale to ensure that ski bindings world-wide release under the same force. Those of us who fail to change the settings as we get older are considered to be guilty of "din sin."

Fall line: The straightest and steepest line down any slope. Also used to describe the line water would follow if poured down the slope.

Finitiation: When the end of one turn seamlessly leads to the beginning of the next. Applicable to both life and snow sports.

Green circles, blue squares, and black diamonds: The markings used to indicate the difficulty of a mountain's slopes. Greens are easiest, blues moderate or intermediate and blacks advanced. A double black diamond indicates the toughest run.

Powder: Light, ungroomed snow.

Snowprioception: the ability to perceive your body's position and alignment while moving on snow.

Telemark: A turn in which the skier's heel is not attached to the ski; the outside ski is advanced considerably ahead of the other ski and then turned inward at a steadily widening angle until the turn is completed.

Exercise Science Terms

Core-dination: Incorporating balance skills to insure coordinated movement

Core-Essentials: the basic balance and postural alignment skills needed to perform the Snow Condition Workout.

Core Muscles: The deep supporting muscles comprised of the:

- Multifidus—A deep muscle running from the neck to the lumbar spine. About two thirds of your lumbar support is produced through contraction of the multifidus muscle.

- Interspinales, Intertransversari, and Rotatores—These structures connect to the spinal column. They are important for rotary movement and lateral stabilization.

- Internal/External Obliques & Transversus Abdominus—The compressive force exerted by these muscles creates the intra-abdominal pressure necessary for spinal stability.

- Erector Spinae—These muscles help to balance all the forces involved in spinal flexion.

- Quadratus Lumborum—This muscle is responsible for stabilizing the 12th rib during respiration and lateral flexion of the trunk.

- Transverse Abdominal Muscle—The transverse is the deepest of the six abdominal muscles. It extends between the ribs and the hips and wraps around the center of the trunk from front to back.

Concentric Muscle Contraction: A contraction that occurs when your muscle contracts and shortens at the same time.

Eccentric Muscle Contraction: A contraction that occurs when your muscle contracts and lengthens at the same time.

Kinetic Chain: An interconnected system designed to absorb, distribute and produce forces throughout the body.

Plyometric Exercise: An exercise that involves an eccentric muscle contraction quickly followed by a concentric muscle contraction.

Pronation: Rotation of the medial bones of the midtarsal region of the foot inward and downward so that in walking the foot tends to come down on its inner margin.

Proprioception: The neurological sense that allows you to know not only where you are in space, but also the position and location of each individual body part and joint.

Snow Condition Workout: A progressive exercise program designed to enhance the athletic skills needed for snow sports.

Miscellaneous Terms and Names

ACL: (ACL) The anterior cruciate ligament connects the femur to the tibia at the center of the knee. It is responsible for limiting rotation and forward motion of the tibia.

Dr. Barry L. Seiller: Ophthalmologist and the founder/director of the Visual Fitness Institute. Because of his recognition of the relationship between vision, sports, reading, and head injuries, he created the institute in 1989. Dr. Seiller has authored a textbook chapter on head injuries and visual skills. In 1992 he was chosen as one of three eye doctors that staffed the first Olympic Vision Center in Alberville, France. This led him to accept the position of the Director of Visual Performance for the U.S. Ski & Snowboard Team.

Paul Chek: By treating the body as a whole system and finding the root cause of a problem, Chek caused a major evolution in the fitness industry. Many professional athletic teams use his cutting-edge training methods, and he is an important player in the sport fitness movement.

Title IX: Title IX of the Education Amendments of 1972 prohibits discrimination on the basis of sex in educational programs and activities at educational institutions that receive federal funds. Unfortunately, some women were already well into their college years by the time the law was passed.

APPENDIX ONE

Home Exercise Equipment for Snow Sport Fitness

Some people prefer to do their snow-sport conditioning in the privacy of their own homes. If you have enough space, this can be an ideal situation. Think wisely, however, before you invest in any form of home gym equipment. You do not want to end up with an expensive coat rack.

Many factors should be considered when choosing the right home exercise equipment to suit your particular snow sport.

- **Cost:** While this is definitely a factor, being penny wise and pound-foolish is inadvisable. Low cost equipment is often poorly made. Be sure to consider the warranty when purchasing exercise equipment.

- **Space limitations:** Can the product be folded for storage. Can it be placed where it won't be blocking household furniture?

- **Child and Pet Safety:** Children and pets like to play with cables and rubber products. Is there a way to keep the equipment out of reach of your two-legged and four-legged children?

- **Versatility:** Products that can only be used for a few muscle groups or for one aspect of fitness will soon be subject to the "boredom factor."

- **Sport Specific:** Examine the movements of your sport. How well does the equipment simulate them? Will it train the muscles need for your sport?

- **Training Other Muscle Groups:** This is something you may not have thought about. If you are only using some muscles and movement patterns in your sport, others may atrophy. In Vancouver, the Twist Conditioning specialists discovered that many ski racers are having disc problems because of excessive time spent in the flex position used in the skier's tuck. They train their ski racers to work in extension to balance muscle groups. Keep in mind, although you may wish you can perform your sport constantly, but you do perform other movements. Make sure your body is trained to support them.

- **Portability:** If you like to take your equipment on the road, your options are a bit more limited. Bands and deflatable products such as the stability ball are probably the best option. Your choice depends upon how much you travel. If you only go away once a year, there is no need to choose equipment based on portability. On the other hand, frequent business travelers may want to choose portable equipment.

- **Usability for family and roommates:** Your equipment choice becomes less expensive when family members and roommates also use it. Just make sure you don't end up competing for time on the equipment.

As with all exercise programs always check with your doctor if you have any injuries or health related issues. Play safe and enjoy!

EXERCISE BALLS

Exercise balls are probably the one of the most economical, portable and versatile forms of home exercise equipment. They are also referred to as stability balls, fitballs, balance balls and gymballs. Prices range from ten to forty dollars, depending on the quality. The higher-priced balls usually have a burst resistant property. Working out on an exercise ball requires active deep core muscles. This makes them excellent for developing the balance needed for athletic performance enhancement.

Virtually every body part can be exercised on the ball; abs, glutes, legs and upper body. Resistance tubes can be used in conjunction with the ball for added challenge. Many people sit on a ball when they are working at their computer in order to promote better postural alignment. The balls are inflatable and deflatable, which means that you can take them along on vacation.

RESISTANCE TUBES AND BANDS

Contrary to popular belief, exercise tubes and bands are not just for beginners. They come in varying resistances, some of which are downright challenging. The price is also right. Bands and tubes range from five to twenty-five dollars. Many tubing exercises can give resistance on both phases of movement; concentric, which is where the muscle shortens, and eccentric, where the muscle lengthens. This makes the exercise doubly effective.

BOSU

The Bosu is a favorite training product for the U.S. ski team. The word Bosu means "both sides up." Exercises can be performed with either the dome or platform side facing upward. Peter Twist, sport-conditioning specialist for the Vancouver Canucks, has developed a set of six Bosu sport videos:

- *Bosu for Football*
- *Bosu for Golf*
- *Bosu for Hockey*
- *Bosu for Skiing/Snowboarding*
- *Bosu for Tennis*
- *Bosu for Soccer*

PRO FITTER

The Pro Fitter 3D Trainer is a lateral trainer designed by former Canadian Olympic speed skier Louis Stack. It has been used by sport teams and in rehabilitation clinics. The Pro Fitter costs approximately $450.

SKIER'S EDGE

The Skier's Edge is also a lateral training device, but with more bells and whistles than the Pro Fitter, and at a considerably higher price. The company makes different models for different types of skiing. Sorting out which one is best is an exercise in itself.

- Classic Parallel Carver teaches lateral weight transfer.
- All Mountain Master has six adjustable stance positions.
- Powder/Mogul Master has your feet close on a single platform to mimic mogul skiing
- Black Diamond helps you develop single leg balance
- Rapid Performance Machine has eight different stance positions to mimic various racing forms.
- World Cup Power Plyometric Series is geared for the serious ski racer. It has a steeper ramp angle than the other models, as well as an adjustable power band for added resistance.

TOTAL GYM

Like the Skier's Edge, Total Gym has many products that come in a wide range of prices. The Total Gym is a dynamic pulley system set up on an inclined glide board. Exercises can be done either from the incline or decline position. The machines have varying levels of calibrated resistance, representing a proportion of the user's body weight. The pulley system enables you to perform exercises in three planes of movement without any restrictions on range of motion. This makes it ideal for sports conditioning. The Total Gym Web site has an exercise library featuring over one hundred exercises. For an additional monthly fee you can opt to join totalgym.com and receive a customized workout plan.

A unique feature of the Total Gym is the Pilates Accessory Package. Unlike the traditional Pilates Reformer, the Pilates exercises on Total Gym can be done either in an incline or decline position. Pilates training focuses on core conditioning and postural alignment. It develops strength and flexibility simultaneously. Many professional athletes and dancers are avid Pilates enthusiasts.

THE VASA TRAINER

The Vasa Trainer is similar to the Total Gym. Rob Sleamaker, a sports physiologist who worked with Olympic cross-country skiers, designed it in the 1980s. When ski-skating (freestyle) technique became popular, additional training was needed for the skiers' upper bodies.

Sleamaker was also training professional triathletes, and wanted to develop a way to help them swim better. He developed the Vasa Trainer to help cross-country skiers strengthen their double poling techniques and swimmers improve their strokes.

The Vasa Trainer features the Vasa Ergometer, providing "variable wind resistance that feels like water." The electronic monitor measures time, distance, stroke rate, force and watts. The Vasa Trainer website features links to over two hundred exercises. Like the Total Gym, there are many models to choose from, each with different features.

BOWFLEX

The Bowflex is another cable/pulley system. Like the Vasa Trainer and the Total Gym, there are many types of Bowflex machines, but the Bowflex seems to focus on more traditional movements, like traditional gym-based weight training equipment.

Optional accessories include an attachable DVD player, as well as the i-trainer, which evaluates your workouts and tracks your progress. Bowflex has also jumped on the Pilates bandwagon. Personal trainer and Pilates Professional June Kahn designed this system, which uses the stability ball along with the Bowflex equipment.

URBAN REBOUNDER

Although many professional athletes train on trampolines, spatial and safety issues make them questionable for home use. If you enjoy jump training, but your knees cannot withstand the hard surfaces used in traditional plyometrics, you might consider the Urban Rebounder.

Urban Rebounding involves jumping only a few inches from the surface. There is a strong emphasis on the landing phase of the movement. This is highly important to athletes, because proper landing technique can prevent injuries. The company produces a smaller model of the rebounder for home use. In addition to cardiovascular training, there are some interesting abdominal and upper body plyometric exercises that can be performed on the rebounder. Upper body resistance can also be added by using one pond sand weights. The Sport Specific Urban Rebounding video features movements that simulate various sports.

APPENDIX TWO

For Additional Information

EQUIPMENT, BOOKS, VIDEOS AND PROFESSIONAL TRAINING

The following companies feature equipment, books, videos and professional training for anyone interested in snow sport fitness:

Body Rolling

yamunabodyrolling.com: If you want to purchase the body rolling balls featured in chapter fourteen or take a body rolling workshop, this is the place to go.

Fitour

fitour.com: If you are not quite ready for the time and financial commitment involved in an NASM certification, consider the Fitour two-day *Functional Training Certification*. Learn how to use the Bosu, stability ball, etc. Fitour workshops are given throughout the country. Plan a ski vacation in Colorado, and take the workshop at my studio in Frisco.

Fitter First

fitter1.com: A number of years ago, I had the pleasure of meeting Fitter First president Louis Stark. A former world-class Canadian speed skier, Stark began his company after suffering from a knee injury. These two quotes represent his company's philosophy:

"I believe that quality of life does not come from what you have, it comes from what you do with what you have."

"In an aging population, balance training will enhance the quality of life through improved confidence, agility and performance in sports and daily living. This in turn will help assure that a persons later years will be some of the best years of their life."

After my ACL injury, I used two of their products: the Pro-fitter and the SRF Board. You can contact the company at 1-800-FITTER1 (348-8371). If you are visiting the Banff area resorts, consider stopping in Calgary to check out the Fitter-1 store.

Institute for Human Performance

ihpfit.com: Although Juan Carlos Santana lives in Florida, he enjoys taking snowboard vacations. At his Institute for Human Performance in Boca Raton, he can help you train the skills needed for all snow sports. The JC bands that he created are perfect for many of the Snow Condition exercises.

National Academy of Sports Medicine

nasm.org: If you want to specialize in cutting-edge sport conditioning, this is the place to go. The academy conducts workshops, has scientific and performance advisory boards, offers certifications, continuing-education units, and even higher education at both the bachelor and master's levels.

The Over the Hill Gang

othgi.com: The Over the Hill Gang is an international organization for people over fifty. Throughout the year, they sponsor ski, bike and golf trips to a variety of exciting destinations. Additionally a number of resorts and athletic gear companies offer discounts to Over the Hill Gang members. Some of the local chapters are more liberal about the age requirements. For example, at Copper Mountain, the minimum age for membership is forty-five.

Perform Better

performbetter.com: Perform Better is one of the best Internet sites for sport fitness equipment. They also feature a variety of fitness articles and exercise charts that can be accessed on the site free of charge. If you are interested in becoming a sport fitness professional, Perform Better sponsors *Learn By Doing* workshops and *Three-Day Functional Fitness Summits* throughout the country. Call them at 888-556-7464

Personal Training on the Net

ptonthenet.com: This is the première personal training site in Cyberspace. Expert articles are featured on a monthly basis. A program library comprises hundreds of exercises on various types of balance equipment. Membership gives you discounts on educational workshops, DVDs, books, equipment and more.

Sissel Online

sissel-online.com: Of all the fitness sites on the Internet, Sisselonline has the highest coolness factor. The site features a free, detailed exercise description page. Even better, you can arrange the exercises to create your own custom workout. Sissel-online also features an article section written by fitness professionals.

Ski Clothes

ski-clothes.com: This site has valuable information about ski trips, ski clothes and ski fitness. Sign up for the newsletter, and yours truly will send you a monthly ski fitness article.

Stott Pilates

stottpilates.com: Stott Pilates, located in Toronto, Canada, represents a modern approach to the Pilates method. The traditional exercises have been updated in accordance with the most recent findings in physical therapy and sports medicine research. The Stott Pilates team conducts training workshops throughout the world. They also produce cutting-edge Bosu, foam roller and stability ball videos.

Twist Conditioning

twistconditioning.com: Based in Vancouver, Canada, Twist Conditioning sells sport fitness products and conducts fantastic sport fitness workshops and certifications. Be sure to take a look at their Bosu ski and snowboarding video. If you are planning a ski trip to Whistler, you might want to spend a few days in Vancouver attending one of their workshops. Call them at 1-888-214-4244.

Younger Next Year

youngernextyear.com: Younger Next year authors Chris and Harry have created a Web site that allows members to discuss ideas about staying young. Read my monthly ski articles, and participate in our monthly ski chats.

INSPIRATIONAL SITES

Just as skiing or snowboarding can inspire your creativity, the personal creativity of another skier or rider can serve as inspiration for improving you snow-sliding skills.

Aspect Journal

aspectjournal.com: Aspect Journal is an online publication devoted to ski writing by passionate authors. The content is an exploration of the various aspects of skiing and skiing culture through well-developed storytelling. I think it would be best to let Kristopher Kaiyala describe his Web site: "There is a kind of ski writing that true authors love to create but cannot easily publish in today's market. This kind of writing goes well beyond commercial magazine content. It delves into the deeper aspects of skiing culture. It gives words to shared experiences, joys, visions, humor, ideas, tragedies, anticipations, habits, addictions, and epiphanies. This kind of writing is not assigned by anyone. It comes out of the need to express and create. It is a kind of poetry. A writer writes it because he or she has to. It scratches and claws to get out because it is rooted in feelings and experiences, a person's very existence."

Break Through on Skis

breakthroughonskis.com: For many years, Lito Tejada Flores has served as a technical and philosophical guru for skiers. His inspiring Web site features articles about ski technique, as well as ski-related artwork and poetry.

Bosu Fitness

bosufitness.com: You could easily spend an entire day at Bosu creater David Weck's website. There is a message forum, a section about fitness tips and videos of specific exercises. Be sure to check out the musing in David's blog, where he discusses fitness, life and Bosu philosophy.

Claire Walter

Claire-Walter.com: Travel, fitness, snowshoeing and skiing. You name it, Claire has written about it. She has recently added a Culinary Colorado page, which describes all of the best restaurants throughout the state.

Ski Tales

skitales.com: Ski Tales is a more whimsical site that features ski fiction, poetry, and art work. Kids create some of the content. If you are inspired to submit any work, site owner and editor Julianne Weinmann will send you a free gift.

Winter Feels Good

WinterFeelsGood.com: Everything you wanted to know about snow sports but were afraid to ask.

MESSAGE FORUM

EpicSki.com: With more than 12,000 members from all parts of the globe, EpicSki is the premiere message forum for skiers. The knowledge base is incredible. Got a question? Ask it on EpicSki.

Snowheads.com: This British-based message forum has almost as many members as EpicSki.com. It's the perfect place to hang out if you want information about European ski resorts.

APPENDIX THREE

This One Time at Ski Camp...

When you were a kid, did you love to go to sleep-away camp? Guess what? You can relive these joyful childhood experiences by attending a ski camp. You may even improve your ski skills in the process. Is attending a camp better than occasional one-day lessons? While the answer may be different for each person, there are many benefits to attending ski camp.

- **Camaraderie:** Depending on the length of the camp, you will be with the same group for three to seven days. The support system that develops amongst fellow skiers is helpful for improvement.

- **Consistency:** You will be with same instructor for the length of the camp.

- **Cost:** Most ski camps give discounts for lift tickets. Some even offer food and lodging discounts. Often, some of your meals may be included in the cost of the camp.

- **Quality of Instruction:** Most ski schools use their best instructors to teach at ski camps

- **Common Goals:** Since different camps focus on different types of skiers, you will be skiing with people who have the same goals.

Many factors go into choosing a camp, including:

- Cost

- Length of Camp
- Location
- Instructors
- Type of Camp

Cost, length and location are closely related. A camp may be priced well, but if lodging, airfare and airport transfers are expensive, the trip might be a bit costly. If you only have a one-week vacation, but the camp is one week long, consider the cost of taking vacation days without pay.

A camp may advertise some well-known instructors, but do they enjoy teaching all levels, or only the most advanced skiers?

Perhaps the most important factor in choosing a ski camp is deciding what type of camp you are looking for. Even if a camp is a great deal with great instructors, you will not be satisfied if it does not suit your goals as a skier.

Although a Google search will bring up an infinite variety of ski camps, I had very specific criteria for my selection for this book. I only chose camps that hired top quality instructors. Even more important, camps were chosen for their reputation for promoting a positive attitude.

EPICSKI ACADEMY

Do you wistfully caress your skis throughout the summer? Do you wait with anticipation for every copy of *Ski*, *Skiing*, and *Powder* magazines to come to your mailbox? If so, the EpicSki Academy is for you (EpicSki.com). The academy, one of the best-kept secrets in the ski industry, is a unique concept in ski instruction: it was developed on the EpicSki.com forum, a message board consisting of close to 10,000 ski enthusiasts from all over the world. Additionally, some of the top instructors, boot fitters and ski fitness professionals are regular forum participants. These professionals instruct and conduct workshops at both the four-day event in the west and the two-day event in the east. Past teaching staff has included Eric Deslauriers, author of *Ski the Whole Mountain;* Weems Westfeldt, former ski school director of Aspen; Bob Barnes, author of *The Complete Encyclopedia of Skiing;* and Stu Campbell, writer for *Ski* magazine. (Disclaimer: I am the EpicSki fitness coach—because EpicSki is the Cadillac of ski camps. As part of your registration fee, I'll send you a cutting-edge fitness program.)

A unique benefit of the EpicSki Academy is that upon its completion, you can stay in contact with some of the instructors through the message forum and discuss your progress.

The EpicSki Academy has grown significantly in the past few years. The main event usually takes place somewhere in the Rockies, such as Utah, Colorado or Montana. Additionally, each December, there is a two-day camp at Stowe in Vermont. The year 2007 marks the inaugural Lake Tahoe EpicSki Academy.

SKI CAMPS FOR PERSONAL GROWTH

Thomas Crum: The Magic of Skiing

The Magic of Skiing program with Thomas Crum is an Aspen-based workshop for skiers of all levels. If you are actively seek the extraordinary in your skiing and your daily life, this is the workshop for you. The Magic of Skiing program teaches you to turn your skis like never before. As fear is transformed into power, skiing becomes a revitalizing and enriching experience. Thomas Crum is a black belt instructor in the art of Aikido, an instructor with the Aspen Ski School, and a certified instructor with the Professional Ski Instructors Association. He is the author of *Journey To Center,* as well as a number of other books on personal growth. I asked Tom to describe his own program: "Too many of us have lost touch with the child-like wonder we experienced in life when we were kids. Skiing is a time to let go of our adult dilemmas and enjoy gliding freely down snow-covered mountains. Technology has made it so much easier to play on skis and boards—lightweight clothing keeps us dry and warm, high-speed lifts swoop us to mountaintops in minutes. With the advent of coaches such as my Magic of Skiing team who are versed in not only how to teach skiing and snow boarding mechanics but also how to center, relax, and breathe calmly on the mountain, we all can begin to use this wonderful sport to reach our full potential, both on and off the mountain, with maximum joy and minimum struggle."

For information, call (970) 925-7099, or write to ski@aikiworks.com

Kristen Ulmer's Ski to Live

Kristen Ulmer is a woman who understands the meaning of the word "action." For twelve years in a row, the ski industry considered her the best skier in the world. Today, Kristen shares her passion at her Ski to Live clinics, usually conducted at Snowbird and Alta. She even conducts a special clinic for cancer survivors.

I asked Kristen about the physical, spiritual and psychological benefits she has seen in adult learners of a snow sport. "Skiing and snowboarding are two of the few sports that exist to which people commit everything—they work, eat, sleep and breathe the sport—usually for decades or even lifetimes. And that commitment makes sense, I can think of no better way to express our spiritual source, and the joy of being a human being, than through cold deep powder snow and high speeds, set to the backdrop of fierce, proud mountains."

Kristen's describes her Ski to Live clinics this way: "Skiing and snowboarding aren't just about expensive real estate, ten-dollar burgers and hard partying—even though the ski industry promotes it this way. These sports are, instead, an opportunity to create friendships, laugh your ass off, and most importantly—discover who you are through an unfiltered interaction with nature. At Ski to Live we also take it one step further, and offer a poignant glimpse of transcendent states of being."

Although most of the clinics take place at Snowbird or Alta, she occasionally conducts an Eastern event. The clinics combine yoga, skiing and evening presentations with Zen Buddhist Master Genpo Rashi. The Ski to Live clinic helps you gain insight about how your skiing style can be compared to how you handle other situations in your life. For example, do you often find yourself in the back seat often; giving up on turns before they're finished? It's possible that this attitude is reflected in other areas of your life.

Brilliant Skiing: The Sports Diamond at Aspen

Having worked with Weems Westfeldt, author of *Brilliant Skiing*, I will strongly recommend his Diamond Weeks at Aspen Ski Resort. The Sports Diamond can be described as a learning system for gaining an understanding the sport. I described the philosophies of the method in chapter seventeen. I asked him to give my readers, though, a chance to get to know him a bit better, and he was happy to do so.

"Hi! I'm Weems Westfeldt—an ancient ski pro, plying my trade on the mountains of Aspen/Snowmass. In collaboration with the Ski & Snowboard Schools of Aspen and with Sports Diamond Partners, I've put together a concept of training that offers a new dimension in brilliance for skiers and snowboarders.

"The Sports Diamond shows you how to keep from ever sinking into the ugly horror of the Plain of Frustrations—that plateau of pain where each moment feels like your legs are made of lead, your mind is paralyzed with fear or self-reproach, and your skiing makes my eyes bleed. In its place you will find the Universe of Endless Breakthrough where all your moments are brilliant moments of discovery and growth where you ski like a goddess or a god—with flair and finesse, dominating the terrain with the agility of a mountain goat and the courage of a lion.

"Well... maybe not. But here's what it will help you do as you learn to use it.

"Design a better next lesson with your coach. When your next coach asks you what you want to learn, what you say you want will probably be consistent with what you need.

"Self-coach better in practice or free skiing. Always know where to go next when you begin to get stuck. This makes it self-coaching instead of self-beating.

"Use skiing to amp up other sports. Imagine becoming a better golfer from your ski lesson.

"Make every day brilliant. I've had many days where I've skied badly (even very badly), but I've never had a bad day on skis.

"The Diamond Sessions will show you a simple truth: There is no learning plateau. As a bonus, we'll show you the joy, the jokes, and why we have dedicated our lives (and foregone our livelihoods) in pursuit of these sports."

In addition to the Sports Diamond weeks, managers, teachers, CEOs, etc., can also take the Leadership Diamond Sessions. This program is based on the philosophy that dynamic and effective leadership is based on four distinct principles: Vision, Courage, Reality, and Ethics. These sessions combine leaderships training skills with time on the snow. They are open to skiers of all levels, even never-evers. Weems explains:

"New material, no matter how serious, takes hold more effectively and efficiently if it is fun to learn. The outdoor sessions create a visceral awareness of the material in an engaging mountain winter environment. The indoor sessions expand the understandings developed on snow through in-depth examination of methodology, accelerated 'learning by doing,' feedback analysis and applied learning, using priority issues of participants."

Boomer Beginners at Les Deux Alps!

If you are a beginner over the age of 50 who has become inspired to learn to ski, Charlotte Swift has the perfect program. Beginning in March of 2007, she will present a beginners ski week for people over age 50. The clinic will take place at Les Deux Alps in France, so you can combine a European vacation with a ski trip. Rates will include lodging and half board. Contact easiski.com for details. Lessons are conducted in English.

APPENDIX FOUR

Instructors for Adult Learners

In a perfect world, every ski or snowboard lesson would be a divine experience.

Unfortunately, this is not always the case. While ski areas try to be diligent about hiring processes, some instructors take the job for the free ski pass rather than through any real desire to teach people.

I decided to put my real-life and cyber-friends to task on this topic. I asked who really loves teaching adult beginners. While certification and experience were somewhat important criteria, I was more concerned with empathy. As an interest test, I also required them to ask me to be included, even if I already knew they were great instructors. My other criterion for this list was that they plan to be at whatever resort they are currently working at for the next few years. We all know, however, that life can sometimes throw us a curve ball, so be sure to verify that they are still at the resort before booking a lesson.

Since verbal communication plays such an important role in student/instructor compatibility, wherever possible, I have quoted the instructors' exact words about why they enjoy teaching adult beginners.

THE "A" LIST OF ADULT SNOW-SPORT INSTRUCTORS
Snowboarding

Rusty Carr teaches both skiing and snowboarding at Whitehall, Pennsylvania. He told me he loves working with adult beginners.

Lowell Hart has been "teaching snowboarding for quite some time, and would strive to provide a safe, fun, and engaging session," for any of the readers of this book. Lowell also teaches at Vail, but can provide lessons at any of the Vail resorts, which include Keystone, Beaver Creek and Breckenridge.

Jeff Patterson has been teaching snowboarding for eighteen years. He teaches full-time at Vail at the Vail Village Pod. He is also a snowboard instructor examiner for the Rocky Mountain Division of the American Association of Snowboard Instructors.

Skiing

Bill Aitkin told me that he "started skiing at age forty on a whim. It was my fatherly duty at the time to bring our two daughters to the local ski hill every Saturday. After watching the kids having fun sliding around on the snow for most of the winter, I thought I'd give it a try. I've been addicted ever since. Money being tight at the time and looking for a way to feed my addiction without breaking the bank, I followed the suggestion of a friend and signed up with the ski school as an instructor. When the little hill I started at closed, I moved on to Mountain Creek. The upcoming season will be my thirteenth season as an instructor.

"About half of the lessons that I teach are to adult learners. Having started skiing as an adult I recognize the special needs of adults and understand their fears and concerns.

"The best way to arrange a lesson is to contact the Mountain Creek Ski School. I can be contacted at Bil8ken@aol.com. Please type MC Instruction in the subject line." Mountain Creek, (973) 827-2000.

Kneale Brownson also teaches skiing at Boyne Mountain. I've seen Kneale in action. He looks like Jerry Garcia, but skis as if he weighs one hundred twenty pounds.

"I'll bet at least half the 265 hours I taught last season were adult beginner lessons. While I've been skiing since childhood, I'm sensitive to the struggles of beginners because I'm very much not an athlete and have developed whatever skills I have through considerable practice. I've had a good many experiences over the years with folks who ended up saying something like, 'hey, this really could be fun.'

I have been in cyber-communication with **Larry Cohen** since I first learned to ski. Larry was always willing to answer any question, giving as much detail as was needed. Larry teaches at Seven Springs in Pennsylvania.

Dan DuPree told me that he would be "honored" to be listed. "I've been skiing twenty years, teaching ten years, and LIII for five years. My preference is teaching adults. I actually don't do well with kids, maybe because I'm really just a really old kid myself. I learned to ski at thirty-five, so I have a strong belief that anyone can. Teaching at Boyne Highlands, Harbor Springs, Michigan. Available weekends and holidays. Contact the Boyne Highlands ski school at 1-800-go-boyne.

"I can teach in southwest Michigan at Timber Ridge weekday evenings by private appointment. I could also easily schedule lessons at Boyne Mountain, as it's only twenty miles from Harbor Springs."

Sarah McCourt was so excited about being included that she contacted me twice. "I'm a Level II PSIA certified instructor out of Winter Park/Mary Jane. I *love* to work with beginning adult skiers and the more timid, shy or scared—bring them on. I feel that this is the most 'rewarding' of students as almost all of them want to be there, and if the lesson content is presented in an understandable manner, they can take their newfound sport and make it their passion. This is for most their maiden voyage into snow sports, and presenting it in a positive environment with a *ton* of patience is where it's at for me."

While you are in Colorado, **Katy Perrey** would love to give you a lesson at Copper Mountain. Katey is a great teacher with a fabulous sense of humor.

If you find yourself in Maine, check out **Barbara Schneider**. "I started skiing at four; at eighteen, I tore an ACL and had a reconstruction the old-fashioned way. I kept skiing. I injured my knee again at twenty-five and gave up downhill in favor of Nordic skiing. At forty, I said, what the heck, if I hurt my knee again, I could give up sports. I took to it with a passion this time around, probably because I was in better shape as a result of Pilates classes.

"I teach at a small hill in Maine called Lost Valley. Since I had to make the change from long, straight skis to short, shaped skis, I think I'm pretty good at teaching adults who are returning to skiing after a hiatus or women who are trying to learn quickly because their boyfriends are taking them away for a week-long trip.

"I do a lot of cross training—I lift three times a week, do Pilates and yoga, work out with a Swiss ball, and run pretty diligently. But the thing that I've found to be most beneficial for my skiing has been my horseback riding, which is great for balance, dorsi flexion, confidence and rhythm."

My Aussie friend Janice, who is probably the most critical person I know when it comes to ski instructors, had nothing but praise for **Roger Systad** at Whistler:

"Roger rules . . . patient, listens to client, knows his stuff and can *ski!* When I get nervous, *this* is the quiet voice I hear in my head. *This* is the voice that tells me how to handle the ice/crud/deep soft stuff . . . This is the person I 'see' when I want to imagine skiing with finesse.

"Others may explain the technical stuff better . . . but Roger is the master at getting you to *ski* . . . gentle, subtle, never rude like some arrogant instructor types that think they are god's gift to skiing and ski instruction—Roger is *always* a gentleman and a *gentle* man. Probably the instructor I trust the most."

Ron White, who teaches at Ski Windham, was very enthusiastic about this project: "I do the instructor training at my area for first time beginners and, having taught for twenty-eight years, have taught thousands in the age group you are describing. The beginner progression I have developed and implemented in our ski school is very different from anything I have ever seen and is very effective."

Index

About the Author

Lisa Marie Mercer began her fitness career in New York City in the 1970s. Highlights of her fitness career include teaching fitness for the chorus of the Metropolitan Opera and working as a professional belly dancer at various clubs and restaurants. While studying Italian at the Universita di Stranieri in Perugia, Italy, she taught fitness classes to international students. When she and her husband attended a Global Unity conference at a castle outside of Prague, Lisa taught fitness to conference attendees.

In addition to attending a diverse multitude of fitness instructor training workshops and certifications, Lisa supplemented her fitness training with dance classes at Alvin Ailey, Martha Graham, and Luigi. When she and her husband moved to Boston, she learned to ski. In Boston, Lisa taught at various corporate and private facilities, including Emerson College, Northeastern University, and WellSpace, a holistic health center in Cambridge.

A few years after learning to ski, Lisa, her husband Mark, their greyhound Giselle, and their cats, Willow and Blackcomb, moved to Summit County Colorado, where they are co-owners of Mountain Sport Pilates and Fitness in Frisco. She is also a Master Instructor Trainer for Fitour, a national certification organization. During the winter, Mark teaches skiing at Breckenridge, and Lisa works as a skier surveyor at Copper Mountain. She is the ski fitness expert for the prestigious EpicSki Academy and for ski-clothes.com, as well as the ski expert for YoungerNextYear.com. *Ski Magazine* has cited her as a ski fitness expert.

When she's not teaching fitness, Lisa works as a freelance writer. Her work has been published in the *Professional Skier, HerSports, Aspen Magazine,* and other print and online publications. Having traveled extensively throughout North America, Europe, Great Britain, the Caribbean and the Middle East, Lisa uses her travel expertise to write articles for travel websites. She occasionally takes acting classes and has performed at shows at the Backstage Theatre in Breckenridge.

Be sure to check out additional titles from the

OPEN YOUR HEART series

and *Dream Time* PUBLISHING

Available now at
www.dreamtimepublishing.com

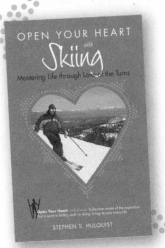

Also in the
OPEN YOUR HEART series

OPEN YOUR HEART with SKIING
OPEN YOUR HEART with WRITING
OPEN YOUR HEART with TENNIS
OPEN YOUR HEART with SINGING
OPEN YOUR HEART with PETS
OPEN YOUR HEART with GEOCACHING

Visit **www.dreamtimepublishing.com** for details
and to sign up for contests, updates, and additional information.